Essential Microsoft® Windows® 2000 Professional

Essential Microsoft® Windows® 2000 Professional

A Desktop User's Guide

Jerry Lee Ford, Jr.

Authors Choice Press

San Jose New York Lincoln Shanghai

Essential Microsoft® Windows® 2000 Professional
A Desktop User's Guide

Authors Choice Press
an imprint of iUniverse.com, Inc.

For information address:
iUniverse.com, Inc.
5220 S 16th, Ste. 200
Lincoln, NE 68512
www.iuniverse.com

Microsoft and Microsoft Windows are
trademarks of Microsoft Corporation.

ISBN: 0-595-17102-8

Printed in the United States of America

To my best friends:

Mike, Mark and Nick.

Long live the Inner IV.

CONTENTS

ACKNOWLEDGEMENTS

I would like to thank my mother, Martha Ford, for lending me her considerable talents and proofreading skills on yet another project.

INTRODUCTION

Essential Microsoft Windows 2000 Professional: A Desktop User's Guide is designed as a quick start guide for Windows 2000 Professional. It was written so you can get up and running quickly without having to dedicate the time required to read through a 500-800 page manual just so you can learn how to turn your computer on. Topics are presented in a concise step-by-step fashion, with a focus on how to perform the most common tasks such as organizing your desktop, installing and running applications and performing basic administrative tasks.

This book is not a comprehensive administrator reference manual. It leaves topics such as networking, advanced security and systems management to other books and provides you with a guide targeted at how to perform tasks that are relevant to everyday users. This book provides you with a comprehensive overview of Windows 2000 Professional from the perspective of the end user without the technical overhead that you do not want or need.

Whether you are new to computers or have some experience with other Microsoft operating systems, *Essential Microsoft Windows 2000 Professional: A Desktop User's Guide* will provide you with the information you need to start getting value out of your new operating system right away.

Readership For This Book

Essential Microsoft Windows 2000 Professional: A Desktop User's Guide is a quick start guide written for the beginning or intermediate computer user who is currently working Windows 95, Windows 98, Windows ME, or Windows NT Workstation and needs to learn how to work Windows 2000 Professional. But even if you are completely new to computing, you will find the material presented in this book provides an excellent starting point.

Conventions Used in This Book

In order to make Upgrading to Windows 2000 Professional easer to read and understand, the following conventions have been used.

- **Bold.** Used to point out where you will need to provide information, click on an option or to place extra emphasize on certain text.

- Underlined. Used to identify keyboard shortcuts on menus and dialog boxes

In addition to the above conventions, this book makes liberal use of two other techniques for directing subject matter to your attention as outlined below:

Note: *Used to provide additional information or further insight on a topic.*

Tip!   *Used to provide information that, while not necessarily essential to the topic, offers advice that can help you save time or get additional benefit from a Windows 2000 feature.*

CHAPTER 1

Getting Started With Windows 2000 Professional

If you are like me you get very excited every time a really good toy comes along. Windows 2000 Professional is one such toy. *Windows 2000 Professional* is the successor to *Windows NT Workstation 4.0*. Originally named *Windows NT Workstation 5.0*, Microsoft renamed it to reflect its new view of the powerful desktop operating system. It used to be that engineers and power users worked with Windows NT Workstation and everybody else worked with Windows 95 or Windows 98. Microsoft heavily marketed Windows NT to the corporate world and Windows 98 to the home users. However, even in the business community, Microsoft found large portions of its customer base sticking with Windows 95 and Windows 98.

Microsoft hopes to change all this with Windows 2000 Professional. Windows 2000 Professional delivers the best of three worlds.

- **Best of Windows NT Workstation 4.0.** Windows 2000 Professional incorporates Windows NT's security and reliability as well as support for such things as NT's advanced NTFS file system, multiple processors and fault tolerance.

- **Best of Windows 98.** Windows 2000 Professional delivers features such as automatic IP addressing, plug and play and the device manager that are standard Windows 98 tools.

- **Integration with the newest technologies.** Windows 2000 Professional delivers a host of new features including the highest level of integration with Windows 2000 Server, modem sharing, an encrypted files system and support for the latest generation of hardware such as the universal serial bus.

If everything goes as Microsoft plans Windows 2000 Professional will become the corporate desktop of choice. With the addition of plug and play support and a simplified user interface that very closely resembles Windows 98, you can bet that Windows 2000 Professional will find its way into many homes as well.

Note: *As of the writing of this book Microsoft has released its newest desktop operating system called Windows Millennium or Windows ME. Whereas the primary target market for Windows 2000 Professional is the corporate user, this new operating system is targeted at the home consumer. However, as was the case with Windows 98 and Windows NT Workstation, you can expect to see a lot of market crossover between these two operating systems. Windows ME is an upgrade of the Windows 98 operating system although it will incorporate some of the newer features found in Windows 2000 such as the My Network places and the personalized Start menu. According to Microsoft, Windows ME will be the last operating system based on the Windows 95 kernel, and all future operating systems will be based on Windows NT.*

Windows 2000 Professional Features and Capabilities

Windows 2000 Professional makes great strides past Windows NT Workstation 4 by delivering a host of new features and capabilities while at the same time simplifying their presentation. From top to bottom, this new operating system outshines its predecessor. Best of all it is even easier to use than Windows 98. Among Windows 2000's strong points are:

*   Stronger security
*   More intuitive graphical user interface
*   Better networking
*   Better Internet tools
*   Advanced plug and play support
*   Expanded hardware support
*   Advanced power management
*   Comprehensive systems management

Stronger Security

One of the most important features missing in Windows 98 and Windows ME is built-in support for user and group security. Access to local resources can be attained on a Windows 98 or Windows ME computer by clicking on the Cancel button at the login prompt. These operating systems can share local disk and printer resources over a network and provide you with the option of either applying or not applying password protection over each shared resource. When network users try to access a password protected resource they are prompted for its password. The problem with this security model is that it is only applied to network users because any user who accesses the computer locally gains full access to all the computer's resources. Also anyone who learns of a resource's password can access it over the network.

Windows NT Workstation provides a powerful security system. Local users are required to present a valid user name and password in order to log in to a Windows NT computer. Network users cannot access local resources unless their user name and password are authenticated either by the local Windows NT computer or a Windows NT Server if the computer is part of a larger network. In addition to requiring user authentication Windows NT can also implement NTFS security if that file system has been installed. *NTFS security* requires that network and local users must be granted specific permissions before access to a resource is allowed.

Windows NT controls user access by way of individual users accounts. You can also manage users by assigning them to groups and then managing these groups thus making it much easier to work with large numbers of users. In addition, the Windows NT security model also includes support for security policies and auditing capabilities.

Windows 2000 Professional inherits all the security features of Windows NT Workstation 4 and expands upon them. Windows 2000 provides the NTFS 5 file system. One new feature that this file system provides for Windows 2000 is the ability to encrypt files and folders or even entire disk drives. Most important of all, Windows 2000 Professional integrates better than any other operating system on Microsoft networks.

Note: *I think this is a good place to point out one important difference between Windows 2000 Professional, Windows 98 and Windows ME. Unless your Windows 2000 user account is set up with administrative privileges you are going to find yourself more restricted on your own computer than you may be accustomed to. Some of the things that you will not be able to do include performing account management on your own computer and configuring its network settings. This is nothing new to Windows NT Workstation users and really depends on how security conscious your company is. Of course, if you are working with your own personal computer, this is a non-issue as you will be able to assign yourself all the permissions you will require.*

More Intuitive Graphical User Interface

If you are used to working with Windows NT Workstation, the Windows 2000 interface may represent the biggest change in your day-to-day work. Windows 98 users will find the transition much easier as the Windows 2000 GUI is patterned after Windows 98. Windows ME, which was released after Windows 2000 Professional, has adopted a number of Windows 2000 features, making its interface an even closer match.

After working with Windows 2000 Professional for just 30 minutes, I knew that I liked it and quickly adopted it as my new operating system. One thing that caught my eye right away was that Windows 2000 was always watching me work and adjusting to the way I like to do things. One way Windows does this is from the Start menu. Windows 2000 learns what programs and folders you work with the most and displays them on the Start menu. Programs and folders that you access less often remain on the Start menu but are hidden so that you do not see them. To view them you simply click on the small down arrow at the bottom of each cascaded menu, and Windows uncovers them as demonstrated in Figure 1.1.

Windows 2000 employs several other handy techniques that enhance your working environment. For example, Windows 2000 implements an *AutoComplete* feature that automatically completes file and path names that you have accessed before as you are working in Windows dialogs such as Windows Explorer. An optional *indexing* feature allows Windows 2000 to let you search for files and folders based on an assortment of criteria such as name, date, file type, and size. Microsoft has also added a collection of new toolbars that are highly customizable such as the *Quick Launch toolbar* shown in Figure 1.2.

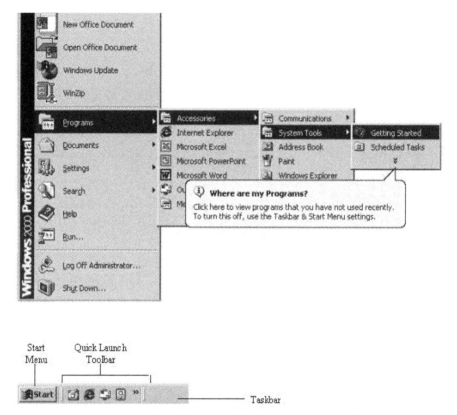

Figures 1.1 and 1.2 Windows 2000 Professional's intelligent
menu system and its Quick Launch bar

Windows 2000 Professional borrows the idea of the *My Documents* folder from Windows 98. Every user gets his or her own My Documents folder. By default the operating system directs all your work to your My Documents folder. This helps you to centrally locate and manage all your work. In addition, Windows 2000 adds a My Pictures folder to your My Documents folder. The *My Pictures* folder lets you view your graphic files without opening them or using a graphics viewing or browser. You will also find improvement in most Windows dialogs. Many of these enhancements will be presented throughout this book.

Better Networking

Although networking is beyond the scope of this book, Windows 2000 Professional is a network administrator's dream. Thanks to the addition of plug and play technology, configuring your computer's *network interface card* or *NIC* is a snap. Simply remove the case, install the card, replace the case and power the computer on. If everything works like its supposed to Windows 2000 Professional will recognize your new NIC and automatically configure your computer to work on a Windows network.

In addition to automating the establishment of an initial network connection, Windows 2000 Professional provides the *Network Connection Wizard* that takes just about all of the complexity out of establishing other types of network connections.

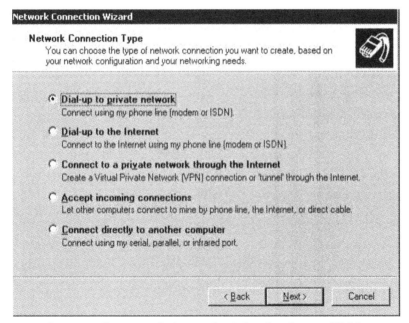

Figure 1.3 The Network Connection Wizard makes establishing
additional network connections a breeze

These other types of network connections include:

- **Connections to private networks.** These are connections to networks other than the Internet. These connections support an assortment of protocols in addition to TCP/IP so that you can connect to networks running different protocols.

- **Internet Connection.** This is a typical connection to your Internet service provider.

- **Modem sharing connections.** These are either connections to private networks or connections to the Internet that have been set up as shared connections. This allows other network users to access a remote network by using your computer as a proxy.

- **Virtual private network connections.** These are connections to private networks over the Internet as opposed to a connection directly into the private networks. Windows 2000 provides several secure protocols that can encrypt your data and ensure secure communications.

- **Incoming connections.** These connections allow other computers to connect to your Windows 2000 Professional computer and access its resources as long as the users initiating the incoming connections have the appropriate set of permissions. If your computer is part of a local area network, you can use the wizard to setup your computer as a gateway to the rest of the network.

- **Direct Connections.** This is a connection via a serial, parallel or infrared link between two computers. Windows 2000 can establish these connections with Windows 95, Windows 98 and Windows NT computers.

Better Internet Tools

Windows 2000 provides a robust set of Internet tools. Many of these are going to be completely new to Windows NT users but that should be familiar to Windows 98 and Windows ME users. In many cases Windows 98 provides these same sets of applications although in most cases it has earlier versions of them. For example Windows 98 ships with Internet Explorer 4 and Outlook Express 4 whereas Windows 2000 is equipped with version 5.01 of these applications.

Note: *Your copy of Windows 98 may not include the modem sharing and automatic proxy features. These Windows 98 features became available with Windows 98 Second Edition that Microsoft released in June 1999.These features are a standard part of Windows ME.*

Among the Internet tools provided in Windows 2000 Professional are:

*   **Active Desktop.** You can add web content to your Windows 2000 desktop. This means you can add what Microsoft calls web channels that automatically post information from special web sites on your desktop. Microsoft provides an assortment of free channels. An example of this feature might be adding stock information to your desktop that automatically updates throughout the day allowing you to work on your computer while keeping a convenient eye on your personal investments.

*   **Windows Update.** Keeping you computer up to date has never been so easy. This utility connects you to Microsoft's Windows 2000 web site where your computer is automatically analyzed, and you are presented with a custom list of updates, software fixes, services packs and updated software drivers. The information gathered from your computer is not saved so confidentiality is assured. Once

presented with a list of updates you simply select the ones you want, and Windows 2000 takes care of the rest.

- **Internet Explorer 5.01.** This is the latest version of the popular Microsoft browser. It features faster performance, easier to understand error messages, automatic correction of mistyped web site addresses, the ability to reuse input on web forms and tighter integration with Windows and Windows utilities.

- **Outlook Express 5.01.** This is the latest version of Microsoft's e-mail and news application.

- **NetMeeting 3.01.** This application provides real-time on-line conferencing capabilities. You can communicate using video, voice and text over your Internet connection and even share applications and white boards with conference participants.

- **Network Connection Wizard.** As mentioned in the previous section, this wizard helps make short work of establishing various types of network connections.

- **Internet modem sharing.** This feature allows a computer with a modem and Internet access to share that access with other network computers.

- **Automated proxy setup.** This feature allows you to use the Network Connection Wizard to search for a computer on your network that has a shared modem and automatically connect to it in order to share its Internet connection.

Advanced Plug And Play Support

If you asked a group of Windows NT Workstation users to list five things that they'd like to see added to Windows NT you can bet that *plug and play* would appear on just about every list. Getting new hardware to work with Windows NT has always been a challenge and sometimes even a nightmare on Windows NT.

Plug and play hardware is designed so that the operating system can automatically detect it. Without this feature, many small companies and home users might find that the process of migrating to Windows 2000 too difficult. However while Windows 2000 Professional does provide a great deal more support for legacy hardware than Windows NT, it is still lacking in this area when compared to Windows 98 or Windows ME.

You may have older hardware that is not plug and play compatible. This does not means that it will not work with Windows 2000. First check to see if the hardware manufacturer provides a Windows 2000 software driver for the device at its web site. If it does then you can manually install the hardware using the Add/Remove Hardware utility.

Tip!   *Microsoft has performed extensive compatibility testing on thousands of different hardware devices for Windows 2000. It publishes this information in the Hardware Compatibility List or HCL. Before purchasing new hardware, check to see if Microsoft has listed it in the HCL. The most current copy of the HCL is available online. As of the writing of this book, it could be found at http://www.microsoft.com/hwtest.hcl.*

Note: *Even with the extensive hardware compatibility testing that Microsoft has done for Windows 2000, it still does not support as many legacy devices as Windows 98 or Windows ME.*

Windows 2000 Professional supports plug and play at three levels:

•   **Plug and play devices with plug and play drivers.** These are devices specifically designed to work with Windows operating systems and which have Windows 2000 plug and play devices drivers. This allows Windows 2000 to automatically detect and configure them and to provide advanced power management.

• **Non-plug and play devices with plug and play drivers.** These are older hardware devices that while not plug and play compliant have software drivers that allow Windows 2000 to provide partial power management. These devices can be installed using the Add/Remove Programs utility.

• **Non-plug and play devices without plug and play drivers.** These are older hardware devices that are not plug and play compliant and which do not have plug and play software drivers. These devices may still be installed using the Add/Remove Programs utility, but Windows 2000 will not be able to provide any power management over the devices.

Tip!   *Just because a piece of hardware is plug and play compliant with Windows 95, Windows 98, or Windows ME does not mean that it will work with Windows 2000 Professional. Always remember to look for Windows 2000 compatibility before you purchase any new hardware.*

Expanded Hardware Support

While Windows NT is sorely lacking in its support for legacy hardware and the latest hardware devices, Windows 2000 is making great strides. While its legacy hardware support still lags behind that of Windows 98 and Windows ME, Windows 2000 Professional has added support for the latest generation of hardware including:

Universal Serial Bus or USB. This is a play and play technology which allows multiple devices to be connected to the computer using a small USB cable. Most computers have two USB ports allowing for a total of

127 devices. USB devices share resources that older hardware devices are unable to share. Examples of USB devices include scanners, digital cameras, joysticks and printers. USB technology supports hot swapping so that you can plug and unplug USB devices without having to shutdown and restart you computer.

- **IEEE 1394.** This hardware standard provides higher-bandwidth connections for devices that require high data transfer rates such as those required by video conferencing. It can provide transfer rates up to 400 Mbps.

- **DVD.** Windows 2000 Professional provides built-in support for DVD drives.

- **Accelerated Graphics Port or AGP.** This technology provides advanced video support and is found on higher end video adapter cards. It allows the movement of large amounts of 3D data between the video adapter card and the computer's memory system.

- **IrDA.** This technology provides for secure wireless communications between two computers using the infrared protocol.

- **Multiple video cards.** This technology is borrowed from Windows 98 and allows you to install multiple video cards and monitors on a single computer.

Advanced Power Management

Windows 2000 Professional can provide varying levels of power management depending on the BIOS version on your computer. On computers that support the new Advanced Configuration and Power Interface BIOS or ACPI, Windows 2000 Professional takes full control of the computer's power management. Windows 2000 provides partial power management on older computers via the Advanced Power

Management or APM BIOS. In addition, Windows 2000 can work with the Plug and Play BIOS during system startup.

Power management is configured from the Power Options utility in the Windows 2000 Control Panel. Among Windows 2000's power management features are:

- **Hot docking.** The ability to dock and undock a laptop from its bay without rebooting.

- **Hot swapping.** The ability to plug in and remove peripheral devices without powering the computer off and on. The operating system automatically recognizes changes in the computer's configuration and manages the power distribution.

- **Smart battery.** Provides better management of your laptop's battery and allows the reduction of power to unused devices in order to extend battery life.

- **Hibernation.** An optional shutdown selection in which all data and application states are stored on the hard disk before the computer shuts itself down. When started the computer loads faster and restores the user's applications and data to their previous state. Hibernation can also be configured to activate after a predetermined period of non-use.

- **Standby.** An optional shutdown selection in which the operating system stores all data and application states in memory and reduces power consumption to hardware devices such as the monitor and disk drive. When the user clicks on the mouse or keyboard, the operating systems restores the system to its previous state.

Comprehensive Systems Management

Windows 2000 adds a suite of new management features that greatly enhance your ability to manage your computer. In some cases these are tools that have been borrowed from Windows 98 or Microsoft's Internet Information Server. The other tools represent enhancements to existing tools or entirely new features that provide significant management enhancements.

These tools give you greater control over application installation and removal and assist you in troubleshooting common problems and performing many typical and not so typical system customizations. Microsoft has integrated a new standard management console that places most of your management tools in a central location and presents a common user interface. This not only makes finding the tools you need easier but also helps to shorten your learning curve.

Some of the more commonly used management tools are listed below:

*   Windows Installer
*   More troubleshooters
*   More wizards.
*   Microsoft Management Console (MMC).
*   Recovery Console.
*   Safe Mode Startup.

The *Windows Installer* works with the Add/Remove Programs utility shown in Figure 1.4 and helps manage the life cycle of your applications. By tracking all the files that make up your application, the Windows Installer can detect if certain key files are missing or corrupted and fix them, and it helps to ensure that application upgrades or removal works as it should.

You will probably never have to concern yourself with the Windows Installer, but I thought you might appreciate knowing what it does and how it works under the covers to make your world run a little smoother.

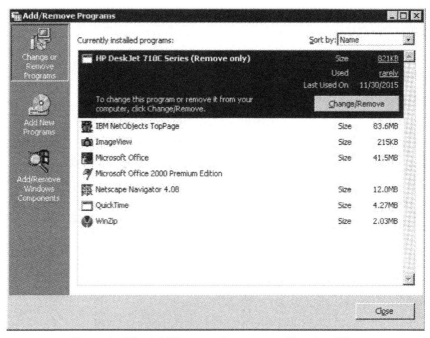

**Figure 1.4 The Add/Remove Programs utility simplifies
the management of your applications**

Troubleshooters help you to analyze and fix problems that occur on your computer. Microsoft has added new troubleshooters and made improvements to existing ones. There are troubleshooters for network communications, hardware, system configurations, remote access, multimedia and sound and for working with MS-DOS 16-bit and Windows 3.1 legacy programs.

Windows 2000 has dozens of *wizards* that are designed to assist you in installing and configuring your system settings, software, hardware, network and Internet connections. These wizards are part of Microsoft's ongoing effort to deliver as many features as possible without overwhelming the user with new layers of complexity. If you make changes on your own computer, then you will have plenty of opportunity to work with and appreciate these handy tools.

The *Microsoft Management Console* or *MMC* is a tool that first made its appearance as part of the Microsoft Internet Information Server application that ran on Windows NT Server 4.0. The MMC is a framework that supports snap-in management tools. Out of the box Windows 2000 Professional provides an assortment of predefined management consoles containing the *snap-in* tools that are most commonly used. Windows 2000 provides an assortment of additional snap-ins. You can create you own management consoles and add in any combination of your available snap-ins. In this manner you can create custom management consoles that best suit the manner in which you work. Figure 1.5 shows the Computer Management console. This is one of the default set of consoles that is provided with Windows 2000 Professional.

Figure 1.5 The Computer Management Console is an example of
the new Microsoft Management Console tool set

The *Recovery Console* is a command line interface that you can start by booting off of the Windows 2000 setup disks or CD. It allows you to perform functions such as start and stop services and write to local disk drives. It can be used to try and fix a Windows 2000 computer that fails to boot up. You can even add the Recover Console as a startup option in your computer's boot process.

Safe Mode Startup is a feature that is borrowed from Windows 98. You can activate this option by pressing the F8 key when Windows 2000 Professional is booting. It provides a series of boot options that allow you to boot your computer and fix problems when it is otherwise unable to start. You will learn more about Safe Mode later in the evening.

Note: The Microsoft Management Console, Recovery Console and Safe Mode Startup features are advanced management tools used by system and network administrators and are beyond the scope of this book.

Comparing Windows 2000 Professional To Windows 98 And Windows NT Workstation 4

As was stated earlier in this chapter, Windows 2000 Professional is the direct descendant of Windows NT Workstation 4.0. It has more in common with this operating system than any other operating system. However, in many ways it looks and behaves more like Windows 98 and Windows ME. In order to make the operating system easier to use, Microsoft based much of its user interface on Windows 98. Windows 98, Windows ME and Windows 2000 are heavily integrated with Internet Explorer, which means that they all have inherited a common set of features such as Active Desktop. Microsoft also gave all of the new features that it introduced with Windows 98 to Windows ME and Windows 2000 Professional. These include such things as the Windows Update utility and modem sharing.

Hardware Requirements

Windows 2000 Professional's minimum hardware requirements are higher than that of any other Microsoft operating system as shown in the Table 1.1. Attempting to run any operating system, including Windows 2000 Professional, on a computer with hardware that does not meet minimum requirements produces an unsatisfactory experience. Trust me, I have tried. If your computer's hardware is not up to par, you are better off sticking with your current operating system.

Table 1.1 Comparison of Microsoft Operating system minimum requirements

Resource	Windows 98	Windows ME	Windows NT	Windows 2000
Memory	16 MB	32 MB	16 MB	64 MB
Hard Disk	175 MB	480 MB	117 MB	650 MB
CPU	486	Pentium 150	486	Pentium 133

Compatibility

When equipped with proper hardware resources Windows 2000 Professional provides the best desktop operating system environment available today. However just because your computer's hardware meets Windows 2000 Professional's minimum hardware requirements does not mean that you should upgrade to this operating system. You still need to make sure that your application and other hardware devices are compatible.

You can check for hardware compatibility using the hardware compatibility list and by checking the web sites of all your hardware manufacturers and software vendors. You can also check on hardware and software compatibility issues at the http://www.microsoft.com/windows2000/upgrade/compat web site as shown in Figure 1.6. Here you will find several excellent resources including the *Readiness Analyzer* that is available as a free download as shown below. Run this program to generate a report of all known hardware and software compatibility issues that could affect your upgrade efforts.

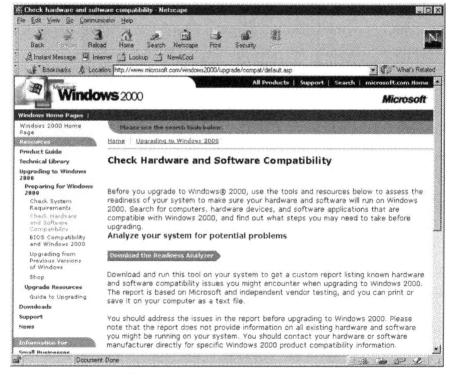

Figure 1.6 Checking your computer's hardware and software compatibility with Windows 2000 Professional

You will also find search tools at this web site that you can use to try and find out if your computer or its hardware and software have been confirmed as Windows 2000 compatible. Even after you have checked with these resources, there is still no guarantee that you will not miss something and still run into problems, but at least they give you a good starting point.

If you are currently running Windows NT Workstation, then it's a pretty safe bet that as long as you meet Windows 2000 Professional's minimum requirements your upgrade will be successful, and all your hardware and software will continue to work. The possibility of experiencing compatibility problems increases if you are currently running Windows 98 or Windows ME. If you use your computer a lot for games, you will probably find that some of your games will not work on Windows 2000. Windows 2000 Professional is the most secure and reliable desktop operating system available, but Windows 98 and Windows ME still provide better platforms for playing games, video and music. If after upgrading you find that some of your applications do not work or do not perform as expected, check the web sites of the application vendors and see if they provide upgrade packs. An *upgrade pack* is a package of software that updates your application so that it works on Windows 2000. If after researching you find that you do have some incompatibility issues with your system, you have several options including:

- Purchase a Windows 2000 compatible computer
- Replace any incompatible hardware and software
- Stick with your current operating system

Reduced Number Of Reboots

One of the traditional inconveniences with any Windows operating system is the need to restart the computer after making configuration changes to the operating system or installing certain applications.

With Windows NT, Windows 98 and Windows ME there are dozens of different scenarios that require you to reboot the computer. With

Windows 2000 Microsoft has gone a long way in making this situation better although there is still more work to be done. Certain management tasks such as the installation of service packs still require a system restart. However, Microsoft has eliminated the need to reboot for such events as configuring network protocols, changing IP addresses and configuring plug and play hardware. This makes the process of changing your configuration faster and more reliable and allows you to be more productive with your time.

CHAPTER 2

Installing Windows 2000 Professional

Before you jump into the Windows 2000 installation process you need to think about a few things. First, examine your computer to make sure that it meets Microsoft's minimum hardware requirements. You also need to make sure that your hardware is compatible with Windows 2000 and replace any equipment that is not.

Next you'll need to decide on what file system you will want to install. File system selection affects the security level and the availability of other advanced features on your computer. If your computer already has an operating system installed on it, you must decide whether to upgrade to Windows 2000 Professional or to wipe out the current operating system and start over clean. Upgrading from Windows NT Workstation 4.0 will produce the best results because this operating system shares a common registry design with Windows 2000 Professional. All of your operating system and applications settings should transfer correctly into Windows 2000. If you upgrade from Windows 95, Windows 98 or Windows ME, you risk losing some software settings. If you decide not to upgrade your current operating system, you will have to reinstall all your applications and recreate any customized setting that you have made.

FAT Versus NTFS

Windows 2000 Professional supports three file systems, each of which provides a different degree of security and functionality. These file systems are:

- **FAT**. A 16-bit file system originally introduced by MS-DOS. Every Windows operating system including Windows 2000 supports this file system. This file system only supports 8 character file names with 3 character extensions and does not provide any security.

- **FAT32**. A 32-bit version of the FAT file system. This file system was introduced by Windows 98 but is also supported by Windows 95 Release 2 and Windows ME. Like FAT this is an insecure file system. It provides for 256 character file names and provides up to 30 percent more storage on large disk drives.

- **NTFS 5**. A highly secure and efficient 32-bit file system introduced by Windows 2000. This file system controls access to files and folders using advanced security permissions that can be managed on a user or group basis. NTFS 5 also provides support for other advanced features including data encryption and disk quotas.

Note: *Data encryption involves encoding the data stored on the local hard drive so that only its owner can access and decrypt it. Disk Quotas restrict the amount of storage space that a user can consume on local hard disk drives.*

Unless you plan to install multiple operating systems on your computer in a *dual-boot* configuration, you should apply the NTFS file system. If you create a dual boot environment and want both operating systems to be able to access the volume where Windows 2000 is installed, then you should use a file system supported by the other operating system.

Otherwise, you will only be able to access the NTFS file system when you boot from Windows 2000 or Windows NT Workstation 4.0.

Note: *Windows NT Workstation 4.0 running with Service Pack 4 or higher can access NTFS 5 volumes. However, support for features such as disk quotas will be lost and files protected with NTFS 5 encryption cannot be accessed.*

If you are going to setup a dual-boot, use information in Table 2.1 to determine what file system you will install with Windows 2000 Professional.

Table 2.1 Comparison of Windows operations systems file support

	FAT	FAT32	NTFS 5
Windows 95	Yes	OSR2 Only	No
Windows 98	Yes	Yes	No
Windows ME	Yes	Yes	No
Windows NT Workstation 4.0	Yes	No	Limited
Windows 2000 Professional	Yes	Yes	Yes

Tip!   *If you are not ready to install Windows 2000 Professional with the NTFS 5 file system, you can always use FAT and then later convert to NTFS 5 using the Disk management snap-in tool.*

Upgrading Versus A Full Install

As I have already stated, an upgrade migrates operating system settings from the current operating system to Windows 2000 Professional, and a clean install means starting from scratch. Migrating is the least disruptive choice. It also migrates your applications and allows you to immediately begin using these applications. However, installing Windows 2000 in this manner prevents you from establishing a dual-boot environment. To setup dual-boot on your computer you must install Windows 2000 Professional into a different folder or disk partition other than the one containing your current operating system.

A clean install forces the Windows 2000 setup process to discover every device on the computer and does not migrate any settings or applications. This means that you will have to reinstall your applications before you can use them again.

Creating A Upgrade Report

You need to make sure that all your applications will work like you expect on Windows 2000 Professional. While Microsoft has gone to great lengths to provide application compatibility with Windows 2000, you may still find some of your older or more obscure programs may not work correctly. You can get information about your applications' compatibility in several ways. One is to visit the web sites of the vendors for your applications. Another option is run winnt32.exe with the /checkupgradeonly option. The winnt32.exe program is located on the Windows 2000 Professional CD-ROM in the \i386 directory. Winnt32.exe is the Windows 2000 setup program. The /checkupgradeonly option tells setup to perform a preliminary check of your system and to produce an *upgrade report* showing any installation issues that it may discover including applications incompatibilities.

If any application issues are reported you can check the vendor's web site for an upgrade pack. An upgrade pack is a set of programs that upgrades the application so that it will work on Windows 2000. If an upgrade pack is not available for one of your applications, you will need to either replace the application with one that is compatible with Windows 2000 or remain with your current operating system.

Tip!   *Don't count on the compatibility report to determine if all your applications are Windows 2000 compatible. The program cannot possibly identify every incompatible application. Make sure to do your own research and visit the web sites of your application vendors.*

Installing Windows 2000 Professional

Whether you are upgrading from another operating system or performing a clean installation, the process that you will go through is essentially the same. You begin by starting up your computer with its current operating system and loading the Windows 2000 CD that should then automatically start the Windows 2000 setup program. If the setup program fails to start you can run it yourself from the Windows 2000 CD at \i386\winnt32.exe.

Note: *If your current operating system is MS-DOS or Windows 3.X you will need to run the winnt.exe instead of winnt32.exe. Winnt.exe is a special 16-bit version of the setup program.*

Note: *If your Windows 2000 Professional computer is part of a Windows network, you will need a network administrator to create a computer account before your computer can connect to the network. If you are upgrading a Windows NT computer, this won't be necessary because the computer's current account name will be migrated into the new operating system.*

There are too many possible permutations to try and cover every possible combination of events that can occur when upgrading from Windows 95, Windows 98, Windows ME, Windows NT or any another operating system. The following procedure outlines the basic steps required for you to upgrade to Windows 2000 Professional from an existing operating system.

1. Power on your computer and wait for the current operating system to load.

2. Load the Windows 2000 Professional CD-ROM. A dialog will appear offering you the opportunity to upgrade your current operating system to Windows 2000 Professional. Click on **Yes**.

3. To upgrade your current operating system and migrate your settings and applications, select **Upgrade to Windows 2000** as shown in Figure 2.1 and click on **Next**.

4. You are presented with the Windows 2000 License Agreement. Scroll down to read the remainder of the agreement and then select **I accept this agreement** and click on **Next** as demonstrated in Figure 2.2.

5. The Windows 2000 setup process displays a window suggesting that you review the information provided at the Windows Compatibility Web site before you upgrade your computer as shown in Figure 2.3. If your current operating system is configured for Internet access, you can click on the **Click Here** option and review the material available at the web site before returning to click on **Next**.

6. The setup process asks if you have any upgrade packs that will need to be applied as shown in Figure 2.4. If you do not have any or are uncertain, select **No, I don't have any upgrade packs** and click on **Next**.

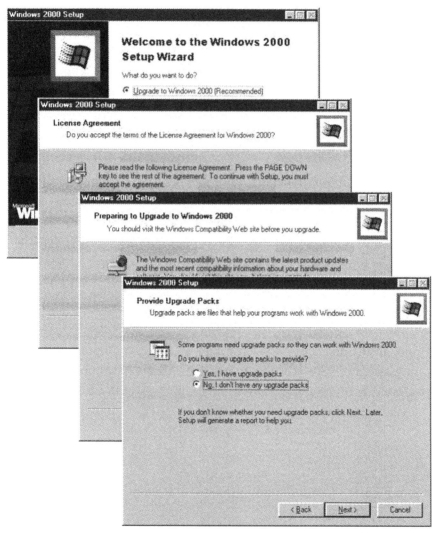

Figures 2.1—2.4 Beginning the installation of Windows 2000 Professional

7. If you are upgrading from Windows 95, Windows 98, Windows ME or a Windows NT operating system using the FAT file system, the setup process asks you if it should upgrade the file system to NTFS as shown in Figure 2.5. If your computer is running Windows NT Workstation 4.0 with NTFS 4 then setup will automatically upgrade the file system to NTFS 5. Unless you are going to set up a dual-boot environment, select Yes, upgrade my drive and click Next.

8. Next setup performs an analysis of your computer and displays a summary report of plug and play hardware that will require updated files as demonstrated in Figure 2.6. You will need to visit the web sites of the manufacturers for the items listed. You have the option of canceling the install process by clicking on Cancel, gathering the requirements and then restarting the upgrade process again this time clicking on the Provide Files button and supplying the requires files or of continuing with the upgrade and getting required files later.

9. The next thing setup does is display an Upgrade Report summarizing any hardware or software problems that it has found as demonstrated in Figure 2.7. Review this report carefully looking before deciding to continue. Click on Next.

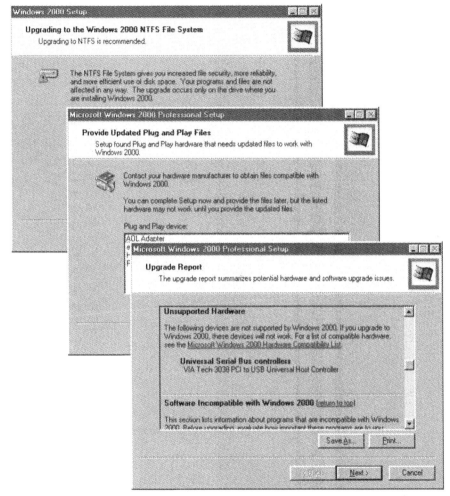

Figures 2.5—2.7 Completing a Windows 2000 Professional install

10. Setup displays a dialog stating that it is ready to copy the files required to perform the rest of the installation from the CD-ROM to the computer and to convert the file system to NTFS. During this process setup will reboot the computer several times. This portion

of the setup process can take up to an hour depending on your hardware. Click on **N**ext.

11. Windows 2000 loads and begins detecting and installing any hardware devices which it discovers. If you are performing an upgrade from an existing system, Windows attempts to migrate as many of your customized settings as possible. What happens at this stage depends on your computer's configuration. If a network interface card is present Windows will automatically configure the computer to join a network. You may be required to provide user name and password information.

Tip!   *If the computer is on a Windows NT or 2000 network and is running Windows 95, Windows 98, or Windows ME, a network administrator will need to create a computer account for the computer before it can actually connect to the network. A Windows NT Workstation 4.0 computer's computer account information will be automatically migrated. To make the install as smooth as possible, make sure that the computer account is established before beginning the installation.*

12. Windows begins its final installation tasks which includes:

  • Installing Start menu items
  • Registering components
  • Upgrading programs and system settings
  • Saving settings and removing any temporary files

Note: *During its installation Windows 2000 creates three user accounts: Administrator, Guest and a regular user account. You were required to supply a password for the Administrator account. By default your user account was made a member of the Power Users group that gives you pretty good control over the computer. The guest account is automatically disabled and when enabled provides only minimal access to the computer. The real power lies with the Administrator account. This account can do anything on the computer including accessing other users' files and changing passwords. Because it is so powerful, it is highly recommended that you do not use this account for regular daily work. Rather you should use your regular user account and only use the Administrator account when you have to. You will find that many of the exercises presented throughout this book will require administrative permissions. If you are not the administrator of your own computer or if you computer is part of a larger network, you may find that you will not be able to do some of the things that you will read about in this book.*

CHAPTER 3

Working With Windows 2000 Professional For The First Time

Now that you have successfully installed Windows 2000 Professional you are ready to begin an exciting journey. But first you need to know a few things about how Windows 2000 Professional works. For example, it would help to know how to log on and off and how to change your password.

This chapter focuses on providing you with these types of information as well as some additional insights such as how the Windows 2000 Professional boot process works.

The Getting Started with Windows 2000 dialog

Having just installed Windows 2000 you should be looking at the Windows 2000 Professional desktop and the Getting Started with Windows 2000 dialog shown in Figure 3.1.

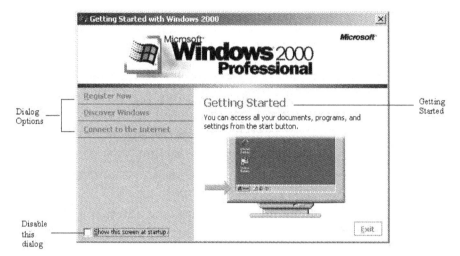

Figure 3.1 The Getting Started with Windows 2000 dialog

The Getting Started with Windows 2000 dialog provides the following four options:

- **Getting Started.** This option is displayed by default in the right hand portion of the dialog, and it reappears any time one of the three other dialog options is not selected. It presents 1 of 6 different helpful instructions which Windows 2000 displays every 30 seconds. You can also click on the current Getting Started instruction to view the next one. These 6 tips are outlined below.

   1. You can access documents, programs and settings from the Start button.
   2. You can double-click on the left mouse button to open files, folders, programs and drives.
   3. Using Internet Explorer and Outlook Express you can surf the Internet and send electronic mail.
   4. You can Access Help from the Start menu to get help on your questions.

5. Using the Control Panel you can customize your desktop and computer settings.

6. You can close windows and programs by clicking on the "X" box in the upper right hand corner of windows and dialogs.

7. **Register Now.** Starts the Microsoft Window 2000 Registration Wizard that is designed to help to register your copy of Windows 2000 Professional via the Internet. This option requires an Internet connection.

8. **Discover Windows.** Presents a guided multimedia tour of Windows 2000 Professional.

9. **Connect to the Internet.** Starts the Internet Connection Wizard and assists you in creating an Internet connection.

10. You can exit the Getting Started with Windows 2000 dialog by clicking on the Exit button at the right bottom corner of the dialog. The next time you start Windows 2000 this dialog will automatically appear. However, if you prefer you can prevent it from automatically appearing by selecting the Show this screen at startup option in the lower left hand corner before closing the dialog.

Tip!   *If later on you want to view the Getting Started with Windows 2000 dialog, you can open it by selecting Start, Programs, Accessories, System Tools and then Getting Started.*

Log Off And On

Logging off when you are done working with Windows 2000 Professional protects your computer and your work. Windows 2000 is a very secure operating system and by default it requires all users to authenticate themselves by presenting a user name and password before gaining access to the computer. Therefore an individual who does not have an account or know its password cannot access the computer or the network to which the computer may be attached.

Note: *When you installed Windows 2000 Professional you were required to provide a password for an account whose user name is Administrator. This account is the most powerful account that can be created on the computer in that it has complete control over the computer and its resources. You were also required to create a regular user account during installation. Typically you should use your regular user name and password when working on Windows 2000 Professional and not the Administrator account.*

To log off Windows 2000 Professional you click on Start and then Shut Down. The Shut Down Windows dialog appears. Select Shut down from the What do you want the computer to do dropdown list and click on OK. The Windows shutdown process takes a while. It is important to wait until it completes and tells you that it is OK to shut down your computer before you actually power off the computer. This allows Windows to write any unsaved data to the hard disk that, if not saved, could cause problems the next time you try and start you computer.

Note: *You can also logoff by pressing CTRL+ALT+DEL and then clicking on the Logoff button on the Windows 2000 Security dialog.*

Tip! *You can add a Log off option to the Windows 2000 Start menu to make logging off just a bit easier. You can turn this option on by clicking on Start, Settings, Taskbar & Start Menu, and selecting Display Logoff on the Advanced property sheet.*

To log into Windows 2000 Professional you must supply your user name and password by first pressing *CTRL+ALT+DEL* at the Welcome to Windows dialog and then typing in your account name and password and clicking on OK. What happens next depends on whether your computer is connected to a network or running as a stand along computer. On a Windows network your login credentials are passed up to a domain controller on the network. The domain controller looks for a matching user account, and if it finds one, checks to see if the supplied password matches the one stored in the domain account database. Otherwise the login is rejected. If the computer is not connected to a network, then Windows 2000 does its own authentication by looking for a matching user account and password in its own local account database.

Tip!   *If you want you can automate the login process by configuring a predefined user name and password using the Network Identification Wizard. Be careful before turning this option on because it allows anyone access to your computer, and if your computer is part of a network, it allows access to that as well. To enable this option double-click on the System icon in the Windows 2000 Control Panel, select the Network Identification property sheet and run the Network Identification Wizard by clicking on Network ID and clicking Next. Next select This computer is for home use and is not part of a business network and click Next. Then select Windows always assumes the following user has logged on to this computer and type the user name and password which you want the computer to use as demonstrated in Figure 3.2 and click Next and then Finish. Restart the computer when prompted. To turn of this option off rerun the Network Identification Wizard.*

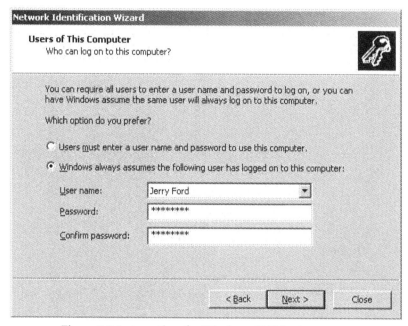

Figure 3.2 Automating the Windows 2000 login process

Working With The Windows Security dialog

Windows 2000 Professional's Security dialog provides a set of tools that help you to secure and manage your computer. To access it press CTRL+ALT+DEL after logging onto Windows 2000 as shown in Figure 3.3.

The Lock Computer option allows you to secure your computer without logging off. This is useful when you only need to step away from your computer for short periods of time. The best thing about this option is that it allows you keep all your applications open and returns your session to its previous state when you return and unlock the computer. Locking a computer prevents other users from logging in as demonstrated in Figure 3.4.

Only the user who locked the computer or a member of the Administrators group can unlock it. To unlock the computer you must press CTRL+ALT+DEL and type your password.

Tip!   *Alternatively you can setup your computer to automatically lock your computer using a password protected screen saver after a period of non-use. This option is configured from the Screen Saver property sheet on the Display properties dialog that can be accessed by double-clicking on the Display icon in the Windows 2000 Control Panel.*

The Log Off option provides an alternative means of logging off your computer. Logging off forces Windows 2000 to close any open applications and files which you may have open. In order to regain access to the system, you must complete a new login sequence.

The Shut Down option provides an alternative means of shutting down your computer. This option opens the Shut Down Windows dialog shown in Figure 3.5.

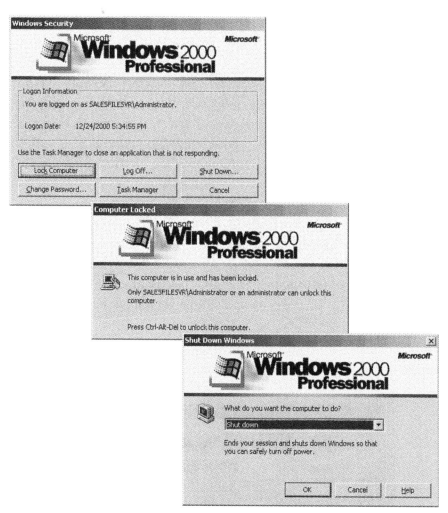

Figures 3.3—3.5 The Windows Security Dialog allows you
to lock and shut down the computer

This dialog provides options to shutdown, restart and logoff of the computer. Shutdown closes all open applications and files, logs you off and then terminates Windows 2000. Restart performs the same operations as shutdown but immediately starts the computer again. You will have to log back on in order to regain access.

Note: *Depending on your hardware and whether or not you have advanced power options configured, there may be two additional options available: hibernate and Stand By. Hibernate allows you to store a copy of all open programs and data on the hard disk. When the computer is later started it restores the programs and data from disk restoring your computer session exactly like it was when you hibernated. This speeds up the Windows 2000 start process and lets you get back to work faster. The Stand By options is similar to the hibernate option except that it stores all programs and data in memory and places the computer into a reduced power state. When you return to your computer and click on the mouse or keyboard, Windows 2000 wakes up and restores your applications and data.*

The Change Password option allows you to change your password. This option opens the Change Password dialog shown in Figure 3.6.

Figure 3.6 Changing your password

It is a good idea to change your password often to protect your computer just in case somebody should happen to figure out your password. If your computer is connected to a network, chances are the network administrator has set up mandatory password policy, which includes forcing you to change your password at regular intervals. If this is the case you will be prompted to change your password during login although you can opt to change it later using this option on the Security dialog.

Tip!   *Your network administrator may also have established a minimum password age policy that prevents you from changing your password until a specified period of time has passed since the last time you changed it.*

Using The Task Manager

The Task Manager option starts the *Task Manager* utility, which allows you to view statistics about CPU and memory performance and to manage active applications. Figures 3.7—3.9 show the three views provided by the Task Manager utility.

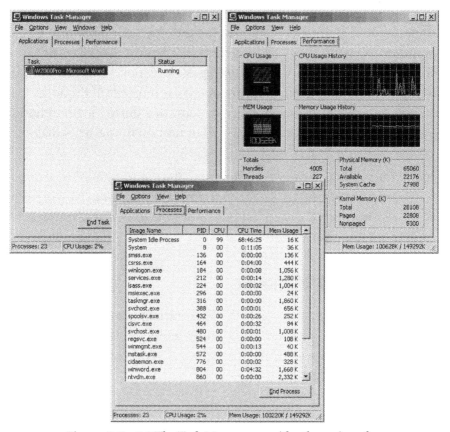

Figures 3.7—3.9 The Task Manager provides three views for
managing and analyzing the state of your computer

- **Applications.** Lists active applications, also known as tasks, and
  allows you to terminate those applications. In addition you can use
  the View menu's Update Speed option to change the speed at which
  Windows 2000 runs a given application. Available options are High,
  Normal, Low and Paused. In addition you can launch new tasks by
  clicking on the New Task button and typing the name of a task.

- **Processes.** List all active processes. An application may run as a single process or may be made up of processes. In addition, there are multiple processes that Windows 2000 automatically starts at system startup and upon which it depends in order to provide basic services. For example, the SPOOLSV.EXE process helps manage the Windows 2000 spooler in support or printing. You can use this property sheet to view active processes, terminate them by selecting one and clicking on the End Process button. In addition you can use the View menu's Update Speed option to change the speed at which Windows 2000 run applications. Available options are High, Normal, Low and Paused. You can also view additional columns of information by selecting the View menu's Select Columns option and then selecting the additional columns of information you want to see.

- **Performance.** Provides a graphical view of CPU and memory usage as well as provides statistical information regarding memory usage. In addition, you can select the View menu's Show Kernel Times option to add a line to the CPU Usage and CPU Usage History views that shows how much of the CPU is being dedicated to operating system functions.

Tip!   *You can also start the Task Manager utility by right clicking on an open area on the Windows task bar and selecting Task Manager from the popup menu that appears.*

The Cancel option closes the Security dialog.

Understanding The Windows 2000 Boot Menu

Part of the Windows 2000 startup process involves displaying the *Boot menu*. This menu displays entries for selecting a normal startup of

Windows 2000 Professional and a special VGA startup mode that allows you to boot up with the standard VGA driver so that you can fix any color or resolution problems. In addition, if you configured a dual-boot environment, there will be an entry for the other operating system(s) so that you can select which one you wish to start.

By default Windows 2000 will be selected if you do not take any action after 30 seconds. You can speed this process up by pressing enter. The information for the boot menu is stored in a file named boot.ini. You can edit the contents of this file to control the default operating system and the amount of time that Windows 2000 waits by opening the Control Panel, double clicking on the System icon, selecting the Advanced property sheet and clicking on the Startup and Recovery button as shown in Figure 3.10.

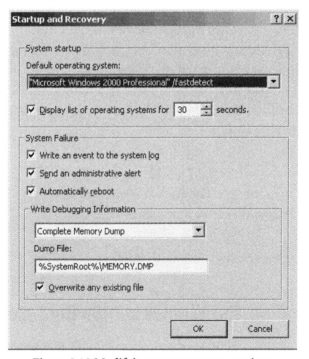

Figure 3.10 Modifying system startup settings

To change the default selection select an operating system startup option in the Default operations system dropdown list. To change the number of seconds that Windows 2000 waits for you to override the default selection type the number of seconds in the Display list of operating systems for ___ seconds field. Click on OK when done.

Operating In Safe Mode

As you work with your computer you may find yourself making all kinds of modifications such as customizing the operating system and adding new hardware. It's always possible you may do something wrong and leave your computer in an unreliable state. To help you deal with this situation, Microsoft has migrated the Boot menu feature from Windows 95 and Windows 98 to Windows 2000 Professional. This feature, shown below, allows you to try and boot your computer in one of several different modes and is useful when you have trouble getting your computer to start correctly.

Windows 2000 Advanced Options Menu
Please select an option:

    Safe Mode
    Safe mode with Networking
    Safe mode with Command Prompt
    Enable Boot Logging
    Enable VGA Mode
    Last Known Good Configuration
    Directory Services Restore Mode (Windows 2000 domain controllers only)
    Debugging Mode

    Boot Normally

Use ↑ and ↓ to move the highlight to your choice.
Press Enter to choose.

You can invoke the boot menu by pressing the F8 key when prompted during startup. *Safe Mode* options allow you to start Windows 2000 using a minimal set of software drivers. Once you have your computer up and running in a safe mode you can try and fix whatever the problem is and then restart the computer normally.

The available options on the boot menu are outlined below:

- **Safe mode.** Starts Window 2000 Professional using a minimal set of software drivers.

- **Safe mode with Networking.** Starts Window 2000 Professional using a minimal set of software drivers including those needed to provide networking support.

- **Safe Mode with Command Prompt.** Starts Windows 2000 Professional's command line interface but does not launch the graphical user interface.

- **Enable Boot Logging.** Starts Windows 2000 Professional normally and records the status of all drivers and services to a file named NTBTLOG.TXT.

- **Enable VGA Mode.** Starts Windows 2000 Professional normally but loads the basic VGA driver in place of the current video driver.

- **Last Known Good Configuration.** Starts Windows 2000 Professional using a configuration that it saved before the last system shutdown. This causes you to loose any changes made since then (including those that may have caused the computer its problem).

- **Boot Normally.** Starts Windows 2000 Professional using its normal configuration.

CHAPTER 4

The Windows 2000 Professional Desktop

Think of the Windows 2000 Professional *desktop* as a work area just like your real desktop at home. Only instead of taking something from out of your desk drawer or desk filing cabinet and placing it on top of your desktop so that you can work with it, you use your mouse or keyboard to start programs and open files by double-clicking on them.

When an application starts up it opens on your desktop. If you start another applications, it opens on your desktop as well. You can use your mouse and cursor to move things around. For example, you might have two applications open at the same time on your desktop and switch between them. Or you might start a bunch of applications and stack them on top of one another and only work one at a time. When you are done working with an application, you can save your work and then close your application much as you might stop writing on your notepad and then put it into a desk drawer.

Understanding Desktop Components

Since you've probably worked with either the Windows 95, Windows 98, Windows ME or Windows NT Workstation 4.0 desktop, you probably recognize most of the features on the Windows 2000 desktop that is shown in Figure 4.1.

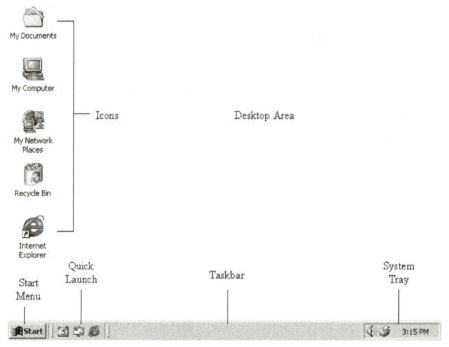

Figure 4.1 The Windows 2000 Professional desktop

There are three main components.

- **Icons.** Icons are graphical representations of Windows 2000 utilities, applications, folders and files. Double-clicking on them starts utilities and applications and open folders and files.

- **The Taskbar.** A bar usually located at the bottom on the screen that contains several features including the Start Menu, Quick Launch Bar and the System Tray.

- **The Desktop Area.** All desktop objects reside on top of the desktop.

Desktop Icons

Windows 2000 Professional automatically places several icons on the desktop. Desktop icons represent several things including applications, folders, files and utilities. A *utility* is a windows component that allows you to manage something such as a printer. An *application* is a software program such as Microsoft Word that you use to do things like create documents. A *folder* is a container that can hold applications, utilities, files and even other folders. A *file* is a collection of data such as a text file or graphic image.

The default set of icons that you will find on your desktop is outline below:

- **My Documents.** Windows 2000 provides you with the My Documents folder as the default location where it will store all your documents unless specifically directed to do otherwise. This helps you keep all your files in one place making them easier to find.

- **My Computer.** Double clicking on the My Computer icon opens the My Computer dialog that contains an icon for each disk drive and CD-ROM drive on your computer as well as the Windows 2000 Control Panel where most of your utilities are stored.

- **My Network Places.** If your computer is connected to a network then you will see the My Network Places icon. It opens the My Network Places dialog that contains icons that allow you to browse your network. From here you can also create new network places that are links to network resources you may use often.

- **Recycle Bin.** When you delete something, Windows 2000 Professional does not usually delete it right way. Instead it gets moved into the Recycle Bin where it remains until you empty it, or the bin starts getting full and Windows empties it. This gives you a chance to change your mind and recover anything that you might not have really wanted to delete.

- **Internet Explorer.** Internet Explorer 5.01 is the latest version of Microsoft's popular Internet web browser. Used in conjunction with an active Internet connection, you can surf the World Wide Web, go shopping, and visit virtual museums and a whole lot more.

Adding, Removing And Deleting Desktop Objects

You may have a few applications, files or folders that you access a lot. One way to make it really easy to get to them is to create shortcuts for them on your desktop. You do this by finding the location of the icon that represents the object you want to access, right-clicking on it and then dragging it from its current location onto the Windows 2000 desktop and releasing the right mouse key. Windows asks you if you want to copy, move or create a shortcut for the object. Copy creates a copy of the object leaving the original object in its current location and in effect giving you a second copy. If you choose this option, be sure you remember which copy is which. The move option tells Windows 2000 to move the object from its current location onto the Windows desktop. Most of the time all you really need is a shortcut. A *shortcut* is simply an icon that provides a link to the real object. Double clicking on a shortcut has the same effect as double clicking on the object itself. You can create shortcuts by dropping and dragging them from an assortment of locations including:

- The Start menu
- The Quick Launch Bar
- Windows Explorer
- My Computer
- My Documents folder
- My Network Places
- The Recycle Bin

When you start installing new applications you will find that many of them offer to place an icon on your desktop during the installation process as well.

You can also create a shortcut by right clicking on an open area in the Windows desktop and selecting New and then Shortcut. This starts the Create Shortcut wizard that allows you to type the path and file name of the object for which you wish to create the shortcut as shown in Figure 4.2.

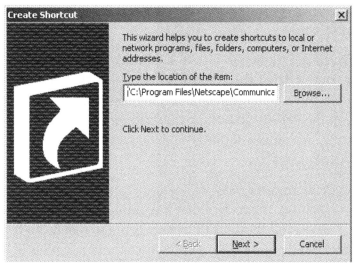

Figure 4.2 Creating a Shortcut with the Create Shortcut wizard

Removing a desktop object is simply a matter of using your mouse to right click on the object and then selecting Delete from the object popup menu and clicking on Yes when prompted to confirm your action. Now remember that in Windows 2000 objects are not really deleted when you delete them. Yes, I know that this sounds a bit confusing, but that's the way Microsoft designed it. Instead of being deleted the object is actually moved into the Recycle Bin. If it sits there long enough Windows 2000 will eventually delete it.

If the document contains confidential information and you want to delete it right away. To really delete a file you must remove it from the Recycle Bin. There are several ways to accomplish this task:

- Right-click on the Recycle Bin icon and select Empty Recycle Bin to delete all its contents.
- Double-click on the Recycle Bin and click on the Empty Recycle Bin button.
- Double-click on the Recycle Bin; select a file, right-click on it and select Delete.

The Recycle Bin is shown in Figure 4.3. In this example the Recycle Bin contains three deleted documents. In the event that you accidentally delete a file you did not mean to delete, you can restore it by either clicking on the Restore all button which restores all files to their previous location or you can select an individual file, right-click on it and select Restore.

Windows 2000 automatically removes deleted items from the recycle bin when it fills up. If you find that it is getting rid of things too soon, then you can expand the size of the Recycle bin so that it can hold more files. Right-clicking on the Recycle Bin icon and selecting Properties, opens the Recycle Bin Properties dialog. Use your mouse to move the slider bar further to the right to increase the amount of disk space that the Recycle Bin can use as shown in Figure 4.4.

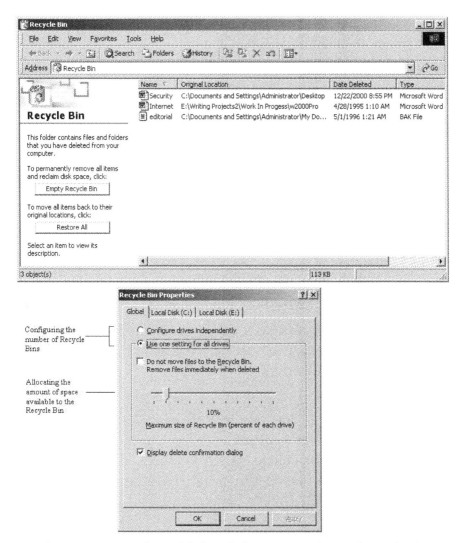

Figure 4.3—4.4 Working with the Windows 2000 Professional Recycle Bin

The following list outlines a few more things that you should know about the Recycle Bin:

• When the Recycle Bin fills up, Windows will only clear out enough room to hold the most recently deleted items. It does so by deleting the oldest files first until it has enough space for the new files.

• If you delete an object that is bigger than the total amount of space allocated to the recycle bin, the object is permanently deleted.

• If you prefer you can tell Windows 2000 to skip the Recycle Bin and permanently delete your files when instructed by right-clicking on the Recycle Bin icon, selecting Properties and selecting Do not move files to the Recycle Bin.

• Holding the shift key when deleting an object skips the Recycle Bin and permanently deletes the object.

• If you delete an object on a floppy disk or a mapped network drive the object is permanently deleted because the Recycle Bin only applies to local hard drives.

• If your computer has more than one hard disk drive or it you have partitioned a single drive, you can choose to establish a separate Recycle Bin for each partition by selecting the Configure drives independently option on the Recycle Bin Properties dialog. You can then manage each Recycle Bin separately using its respective property sheet.

Working With Active Desktop

Active Desktop is a Windows feature that allows you to place web content on your desktop in effect turning your desktop into a web page. You can display your favorite web page as your desktop. You can also setup any picture that you find on the Internet. If you prefer you can keep your traditional desktop and just add web content to your desktop. Microsoft makes a variety of free web content available at its *Active Desktop Gallery* web site. For example, Figure 4.5 shows an example of a desktop with an active weather map.

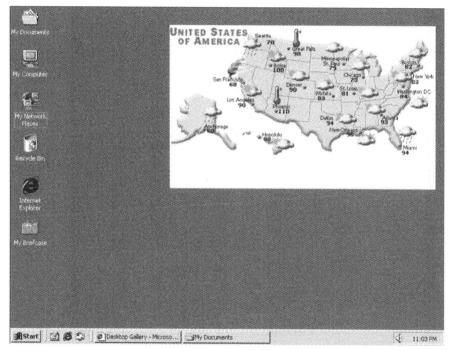

Figure 4.5 Adding active content to the Windows 2000 Professional desktop

Once added, the weather map will display current weather forecasts and will continue to update it as long as it has an active Internet connection.

As of the writing of this book Microsoft's Active Desktop Gallery provides free web content in the following areas:

* News
* Sports

- Entertainment
- Travel
- Weather
- Cool utilities

To manage Active Desktop right-click on an open area on your Windows desktop and select Active Desktop and then any of the following options:

- **Show Web Content**. Enables and disables Active Desktop.
- **Show Desktop Icons**. Displays items on your desktop.
- **Lock Desktop Items**. Locks your desktop content at its current location on the desktop.
- **Synchronize**. Forces an immediate update of your web content.

Note: *You can also enable and disable Active Desktop with the Enable Web content on my desktop option on the General property sheet of Folder Options, which is found in the Windows 2000 Control Panel. In addition, you can enable it on the Show Web content on my Active Desktop option on the Web property sheet on the Display dialog that is also located in the Windows 2000 Control Panel.*

Note: *In Internet Explorer you single-click to access links on web pages and work with various types of web content. When you add web content to your desktop you will work with a single-click as well. However, other desktop objects such as shortcuts, icons and window dialogs will still expect you to double-click when working with them. You can configure mouse click settings so that everything works with a single-click if you want a more consistent feel. Double-click on Folder Options icon in the Windows 2000 Control panel and select Single-click to open an item (point to select) on the General property sheet.*

The Start Menu

The *Start Menu* provides a series of cascading menus that are your primary interface for locating and starting your applications. Menus automatically open as you place the pointer over them. Once you find the application that you are looking for, you can start it with a single click. In addition to providing quick access to your applications, the Start menu also contains the following resources and menus:

*   **Windows Update.** A Windows utility that you can use to automatically find and apply fixes, updates and service packs to your computer via the Internet.
*   **Programs.** A series of sub-menus that let you find and start all you applications.
*   **Documents.** Provides a link to your My Documents folder as well as to files you have recently accessed.
*   **Settings.** Contains links to the Windows Control Panel and several other folders that you can use to configure Windows 2000 Professional.
*   **Search.** Allows you to search for resources on your computer, your network and the Internet.
*   **Help.** Starts the Windows 2000 Help system that includes links to help information stored on the Internet.
*   **Run.** Allows you to start applications and issue commands.
*   **Shutdown.** Allows you to log off, shut down or restart your computer.

You can add entries to the Start Menu using drag and drop. You can also use the Taskbar Properties dialog to add new menus and menu entries that we'll look at in just a minute. You can delete or rename menus and menu entries by right clicking on them and selecting the appropriate option.

Note: *Removing a menu or menu entry does not delete the object to which it refers. It only deletes the Start menu's link to that object.*

When you install a new application the application install process will automatically create menu entries for the application. Similarly, when you uninstall an application its Start Menu should be automatically removed as well.

It Learns The Way You Work

Windows 2000 introduces a new feature called Personalized Menus. *Personalized menus* track the way that you work allowing Windows 2000 to learn the applications you work with the most. It then hides those programs that you do not use a lot from view in an effort to streamline the menu system. You can still get to these hidden applications but clicking on the pair of down-arrows at the bottom of each menu. This exposes any hidden items on the menu as demonstrated in Figure 4.6.

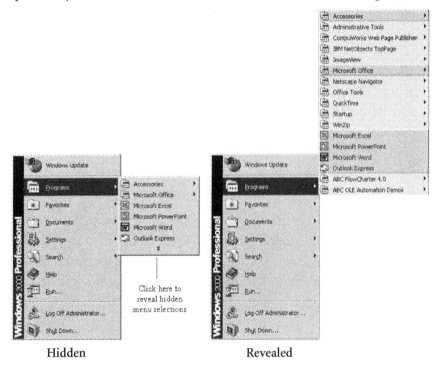

Hidden   Revealed

Figure 4.6 Windows 2000 Professional's intelligent menu system
helps keep the Start menu less cluttered

If you do not care for Personalized menus and prefer to see everything you can use, the following procedure to turn them off:

1. Click on **Start, Settings** and the **Taskbar & Start menu.** The Taskbar and Start Menu Properties dialog appears.

2. Clear the selection for Use Personalized menus and click on **OK.**

The Programs Menu

The Programs menu located on the Start menu is the menu you will access most. This is where Windows 2000 places most of the applications that come with the operating system. In addition, any new applications you install will create their own sub-menus under the programs menu. By default Windows 2000 provides the following when installing Windows 2000 Professional:

*   **Accessories.** This menu contains links for a collection of applications that are bundled with Windows 2000 Professional.
*   **Startup.** This menu is initially empty but you add applications to it. Windows 2000 automatically starts any applications that it finds in this folder during startup.
*   **Internet Explorer.** This is a link to Internet Explorer 5.01.
*   **Outlook Express.** This is a link to Outlook Express 5.01.

The Documents Menu

The Documents menu contains links to your My Documents folder and to files that you have recently accessed. Its purpose is to provide quick access to your documents. To use it click on Start, Documents and then select a Document. Windows 2000 starts up the application associated with the type of file that you selected and then opens up the document.

If you click on the My Documents icon Windows opens the My Documents folder. One trick that may make the Document Menu more useful to you is if you enable the My Document menu to be expanded. This will allow you to drill into the My Document folder and select from its contents as demonstrated in Figure 4.7.

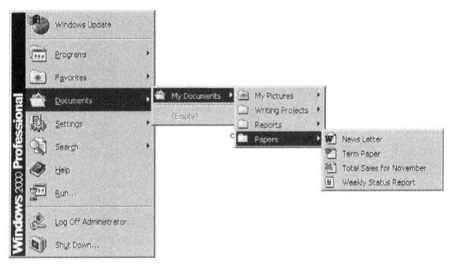

Figure 4.7 Accessing the My Documents folder from
the Windows 2000 Professional Document menu

Use the following procedure to expand your My Documents folder:

1. Click on **Start, Settings** and the **Taskbar & Start menu.**

2. Select the Advanced property sheet.

3. Scroll down in the Start Menu Settings list until you see the Expand My Document option. Select it and click on **OK.**

You can clear out the Documents file if you wish. This leaves the link to the My documents folder while removing all other links to your documents. Use the following procedure to clear out your documents menu.

1. Click on **Start, Settings** and the **Taskbar & Start menu.**

2. Select the Advanced property sheet.

3. Click on the Clear button and then on **OK.**

Note: *Not all Windows programs will add links to your documents in the Documents menu. In this case you must either use a program such as Windows Explorer to find and open the document, open the document from within the application where you work with it or use the Search utility located on the Search menu.*

The Settings Menu

The Settings menu contains links to the following Windows 2000 resources:

* **Control Panel.** Opens the Windows 2000 Professional Control Panel, which contains a collection of configuration utilities
* **Network and Dial-up Connections.** Contains links to the Network Connection wizard and the Local Area Connection Status dialog
* **Printers.** Opens the Printers folders where printers are defined and managed
* **Taskbar and Start Menu.** Lets you manage the Windows 2000 Professional Taskbar and Start menu

The Search Menu

Microsoft seems to be putting more and more emphasis on searching and less on browsing, especially when looking for networking resources. It takes no less than five sets of double-clicks to browse your way down to a network resource via My Network Places. In contrast you can search for a resource by selecting the type of search, typing a search string and clicking on Search.

Windows 2000 Professional supports four types of searches:

- **Files or Folders.** Lets you search by file name, date and type on your computer or local area network.
- **Computer.** Lets you search for a computer on your local area network.
- **People.** Lets you search your local address book or one of many available Internet search services for names and e-mail addresses.
- **Internet.** Makes it easy for you to search the Internet.

The Help Menu

Clicking on the Help menu opens Windows 2000 Help Viewer. The Windows 2000 Professional help system is HTML based and includes links to on-line help on the Internet in addition to the traditional help system. The Help Viewer displays information in a two-pane view.

The left side presents a table of contents, index and search engine and the right pane displays selected help information. The left pane also includes a Favorites tab.

Tip!   *If you prefer a single pane view you can click on the Hide button. This has the same affect as selecting the Hide Tabs option under the Options menu.*

The Contents property sheet displays information in the form of books. You can drill your way down into these books to find subtopics and detailed information as shown in Figure 4.8.

The Index property sheet displays a comprehensive index of Windows 2000 help topics. Simply type a few words or letters, and Windows will display any matching index entries. The Search property sheet performs a search that finds help topics based on the matching keywords. If you find some help topics you think you may find useful to reference again in the future, you can switch over to the Favorites property sheet and click on Add. Windows then places a reference to the topic in the Favorites property sheet for quick reference. You can even type your own description for the help topic as demonstrated in Figure 4.9.

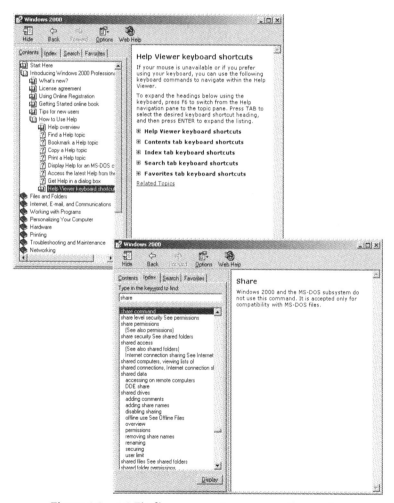

Figure 4.8—4.9 Finding answers to your questions using
the Windows 2000 Professional Help system

The *Web Help* button on the menu at the top of the Help Viewer is a link to the Internet. When you click on this button Windows 2000 displays the Online Support and information help topic as shown in Figure 4.10.

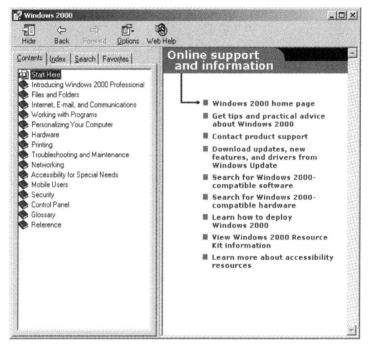

Figure 4.10 Windows 2000 Professional's Help system
provides links to web based help

From here you can select links that take you to various on-line help resources including the Windows 2000 home page.

Note: *If you add a link to an on-line help topic, Windows adds a link to it in the Topics area of the Favorites property sheet instead of its topic title. Of course, you can change this by typing in your own topic description when you add the topic.*

The Run Menu

The Run menu opens the Run dialog shown in Figure 4.11. From here you can perform any of the following actions:

Table 2.1 Run menu options

Action	Example
Open a file	C:\Accounting_folder\January_sales
Open folder	C:\Accounting_folder
Start an application	wordpad.exe
Access a web site	www.microsoft.com
Execute a Windows command	ipconfig /renew

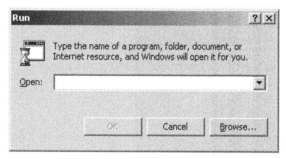

Figure 4.11 The Windows 2000 Professional Run dialog
provides another way to access Windows resources

Tip! *To recall a command that you have recently used in this dialog, click on the down arrow and select one.*

Note: *One thing you may notice when typing in this dialog is that Windows 2000 attempts to offer suggestions as you type. This feature is known as AutoComplete. Basically Windows 2000 remembers every command that you have typed and after your have typed in a few characters, it starts displaying commands that match what you have typed so far.*

The Shut Down Menu

The Shut Down menu opens the Shut Down Windows Dialog that we already covered. So all that I will do here is remind you that it is critical that you never power off your computer without first shutting it down properly. Windows 2000 Professional keeps a lot of data in memory and depending on how busy you have kept your computer, it may not have had a chance to write it all onto the hard drive. Shutting down Windows properly ensures the integrity of your systems and your data. Windows 2000 will display a message notifying you when it's safe to power off your computer.

Working With The Taskbar

The Taskbar is located by default at the bottom of the screen. It contains a number of elements that make navigating around Windows 2000 much easier as shown in Figure 4.12.

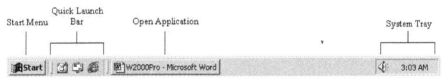

Figure 4.12 You can drag and drop the Windows 2000
Professional Taskbar to any of the four corners of your display

The Start menu button opens the Start Menu and allows you to find and start your applications and work with Windows utilities such as the Control Panel.

Toolbars

Windows 2000 Professional provides an assortment of toolbars that can be placed on the Taskbar including:

*   **Address toolbar.** Lets you type in a URL of a web site. It then starts Internet Explorer and takes you to that web site.
*   **Links toolbar.** Places a copy of all your Internet Explorer links on the Taskbar for quick access.
*   **Desktop toolbar.** Places a link to all your desktop icons making it easy for you to access them when your desktop is cluttered.
*   **Quick launch.** Contains links to Outlook Express, Internet Explorer and your Desktop. You can use drag and drop to add and remove links to this toolbar.

Toolbars are also convenient because they provide you with single-click access. To enable or disable a toolbar right-click on an open area on the Taskbar and select Toolbars and then the name of the toolbar as demonstrated in Figure 4.13. A check mark next to a toolbar indicates that it is already enabled.

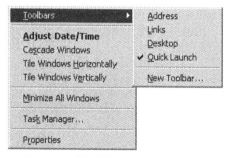

Figure 4.13 You can add additional toolbars to the Taskbar

You may have noticed the New Toolbar option at the bottom of the list of available toolbars. This option allows you to create a custom toolbar out of the contents of any folder that you specify.

Tip!   *If you prefer you can move the Taskbar to the right, left or top portions of the screen by left clicking on a free area on the Taskbar and dragging it to its new location.*

Tip!   *If you have a lot of open applications or have moved a lot of things onto Taskbar toolbars, you may find things get too crowded on your Taskbar. You can increase the size of the Taskbar by moving the pointer to its outside edge, left clicking on it and dragging it up.*

Open Applications

When you open an application such as Microsoft work, Windows 2000 places a link on the Taskbar representing the application. The easiest way to start working with an open application that may be located under other open applications on your desktop is by clicking on its link in the Taskbar. This tells Windows 2000 that you want to work with it again and places it on top of everything else.

The System Tray

Some applications and operating system components place links into the System Tray as well. Left clicking on a link may open the application or it may allow you to work with an already active application. For example, left clicking on the Windows 2000 Volume Control lets you adjust the speaker volume on your computer as shown in Figure 4.14. Right clicking on an application typically allows you to interact and manage the application. For example, right clicking on the *Windows*

2000 Volume Control opens a menu that allows you to view volume controls or adjust audio properties.

Figure 4.14 You can manage many functions of the Windows 2000
Professional desktop using the Taskbar and the System Tray

Date and Time

Windows 2000 displays the current time in the right hand portion of the System Tray. To get the calendar information simply move the pointer over the time field and Windows will display it

If you need more information than this you can get it by either double-clicking on the time field or by right clicking on the Time or then selecting Adjust Date/Time. This opens the Date/Time Properties dialog as shown in Figure 4.12. This dialog contains two property sheets. The first property sheet is the Date and Time sheet. It shows the current month, year and day in the Date section and presents the time in both analog and digital formats.

The calendar presents a view of the current month. You can view or change the computer's date to a different month or year and month by selecting it from the drop-down list. You can change the time by placing the cursor in the hours, minutes, seconds or am/pm fields and clicking on the up or down arrows as appropriate. When done viewing or changing date and time settings click on OK or click on Cancel to exit without making any changes.

The Time Zone property sheet, shown in Figure 4.13, lets you specify the time zone for the part of the world where you happen to be. This information is provided to Windows 2000 during installation. For most of us this information will never have to be changed. But if you move around a lot or are running on Windows 2000 Professional on a laptop and travel a lot you may want to keep you computer's date and time properly set. Windows 2000 records date and time information for every document that you create. If you have ever created two versions of a document and forgotten which version was more current, you can view the date and time stamp to find out.

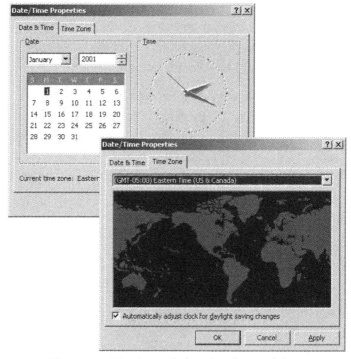

Figure 4.15 Viewing and changing date and time

To change Windows 2000 to a new time zone select it from the drop-down list at the top of the property sheet and click on OK.

Note: *If you decide to take advantage of Windows 2000's support for offline files while you travel, you will want to make sure that you always have correct date and time information. Windows 2000 uses this information when synchronizing files so that it can tell which one is most current.*

CHAPTER 5

Spicing Up Your Display

The appearance of your desktop's color scheme, background and screen saver are among the most fun and personal aspects of computer configuration. No two people have the same taste and so no two desktops look the same either. You can add a little flair to your computer by double-clicking on the Display icon in the Windows 2000 Control Panel and configuring the available options on any of the property sheets:

- **Background.** Place a picture or HTML document on your Windows desktop or fill it with an attractive pattern.
- **Screen Saver.** Pick from one of an assortment of screen savers or add your own.
- **Appearance.** Select a windows color scheme or create your own.
- **Web.** Enable Active Desktop and add web content to your desktop.
- **Effects.** Change the look of desktop ions and configure visual settings.
- **Settings.** Manage color depth, font size, resolution and other monitor related settings.

Tip!   *You can access the Display Property sheet quickly by right clicking on an open area of the desktop and selecting P*r*operties.*

Changing backgrounds

The Background property sheet allows you to personalize your Windows desktop with an image, HTML page or pattern. Windows 2000 provides a collection of background pictures you can select from in the Select a background or HTML document as Wallpaper list. The default is no wallpaper or (none). Windows 2000 provides a mini-preview of each selected wallpaper as shown in Figure 5.1. This allows you to quickly scroll through all of them and find one that is to your liking.

Windows 2000 can use any of the following types of files as backgrounds:

- BMP
- GIF
- JPG
- DIB
- HTM

If you have a graphic of your own that you want to setup as your background, you can click on the Browse button and show Windows where to find it. If your background is not large enough to fill the entire display area you can choose an option from the Picture Display drop-down list to tell Windows how to display it. The available options are:

- **Center.** Places the image in the center of the screen.
- **Tile.** Repeats the image until the entire screen is full.
- **Stretch.** Expands the image so that it fills the entire screen.

Alternatively you can decorate your desktop with a pattern by clicking on the Pattern button. This opens the Pattern dialog as shown in Figure 5.2. Select a pattern from the available list. Windows provides a mini-preview so that you will know what it will look like before you select it.

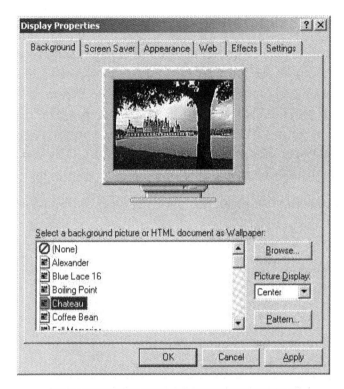

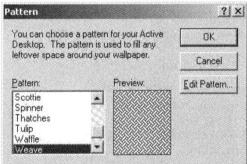

Figures 5.1 and 5.2 You can preview any background or
pattern before you apply it to your desktop

Turning On A Screen Saver

In days gone by the *screen saver* filled the very important role of preventing screen burn-in. When a specified period of time passed by with no interaction with the user, the screen saver kicked in and began displaying interesting patterns, images or cartoons. However, the technology behind monitors has improved much over the years negating the primary function of the screen saver. Today screen savers are usually used for entertainment purposes. Windows 2000 enhances the usefulness of screen savers by allowing you set up password protected screen savers. This added level of security helps protect your sensitive data should you walk away for an extended period of time and forget to logoff or lock out your computer.

Use the following procedure to set up your own screen saver:

1. Open the Display Properties dialog and select the Screen Saver property sheet as shown in Figure 5.3.

2. Select a screen saver from the drop-down list.

3. Click on the Setting button to open the Setup dialog for that screen saver and make any settings adjustments that are desired as demonstrated in Figure 5.4. Click on OK.

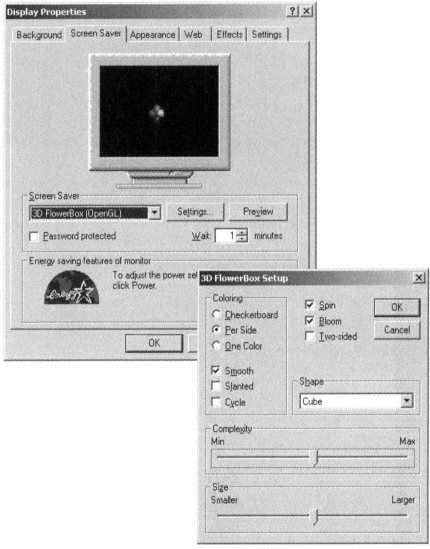

Figures 5.3—5.4 Windows 2000 Professional's screen savers
are highly configurable, and many support password protection

4. Click on the Preview button to tell Windows 2000 to give you a full screen demo of what the screen saver will look like when it runs.

5. If desired, change the number of minutes of inactivity that must pass before Windows 2000 will start the screen saver.

6. If you want to enable a password protection with your screen saver, select Password protected and click on OK.

Note: *Windows assigns your logon id to the screen saver. Once activated the only way to gain access to the desktop is by providing your password when prompted.*

Changing Appearances

By default Windows 2000 defaults to a medium blue color for its background and dialogs title. You can use the Appearance property sheet, shown in Figure 5.5 to change things more to your own tastes. The top half of this property sheet provides an example of how the color scheme specified on this property sheet will look on the desktop once it is applied.

You can make changes in two ways. The easiest is to select from a list of pre-configured schemes in the Scheme drop-down list and click on OK. This option affects appearance of all Windows screen elements.

The second option is to select a scheme that comes closet to matching your preferences and then customize it. You do this by selecting specific screen elements such as the Active Windows Border and then configuring its size and color. If you pick a screen element that contains fonts, then you can configure font size, color, and bold and italic text as well.

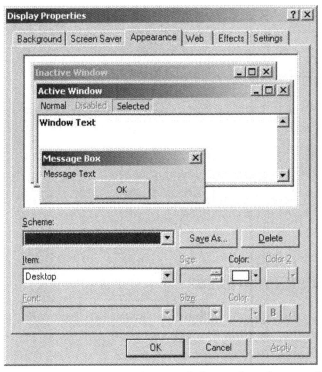

Figure 5.5 You can customize your desktop color scheme and
even build your own custom color scheme library

TIP!   *After customizing a scheme you can choose to save it by selecting
the Save As button. This way you can create a collection of your
own custom schemes..*

Web Integration

The Web property sheet allows you to enable and manage an Active Desktop as shown in Figure 5.6. Selecting Show Web content on my Active Desktop enables support for web content on your desktop.

Now all you have to do is find some web content. To begin click on the New button. This opens the New Active Desktop item dialog as shown in Figure 5.7.

There are three ways of doing this. The first is to click on the Visit Gallery. Assuming that you have an active connection to the Internet, Windows 2000 will start Internet Explorer and deposit you at Microsoft's Active Desktop Gallery where you can select from an assortment of categories. For example, Figure 5.8 shows the MSNBC Weather Map. Clicking on the Add to Active Desktop button instructs Internet Explorer to download the map to your desktop.

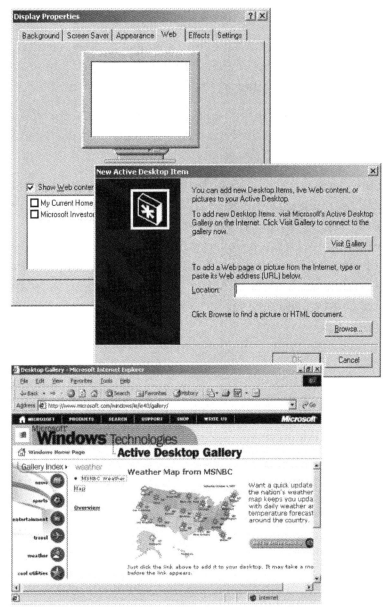

Figures 5.6—5.8 Windows 2000 Professional's web integration
allows you to add active content to your desktop

The second way to add web content to your desktop is to type in the URL of a web site that has either a web page or image that you want to place on your desktop. Finally you can add a web page from your local computer or network by clicking on browse and showing Windows where to find it.

Getting rid of web content is even easier than adding it. All you have to do is select the web content you no longer want, click on Delete and select Yes when prompted for confirmation. The Properties button allows you to view Web Document properties, shown in Figure 5.9, including the location of the URL where you got the web content and the number of times you have visited that web site. You can also find out how current the web content is by checking the Last Synchronization field. The schedule property sheet, shown in Figure 5.10, allows you to specify whether or not you want the web content automatically updated and to edit its Synchronization schedule or create a new one. The Download property sheet, shown in Figure 5.11, lets you specify just how much content you want to download during synchronization and to limit how much hard disk space it can consume. You can even set it to fire off an e-mail every time an update occurs.

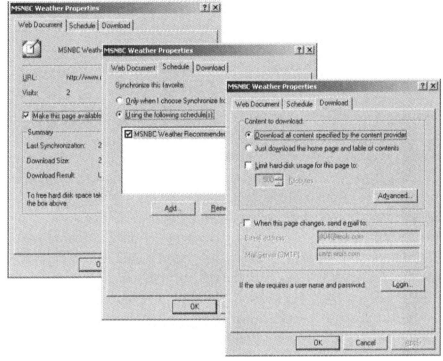

Figures 5.9—5.11 Adding active content allows you to
bring real time information to your desktop

Special Effects

The Effects property sheet allows you to alter the appearance of desktop icons. Simply select the icon you want to change and click on Change icon. Windows displays a collection of icons from which you can choose. For example, the following icons, shown in Figure 5.12, are available to represent your Recycle Bin.

If you do not like your new icon choice, you can easily revert back to the default by selecting the current icon and clicking on the Default Icon button.

You can also control an assortment of visual effects from this property sheet, shown in Figure 5.13, as outlined in the following list:

- **Use transition effects for menus and tooltips.** Turns on animation effects. Your options are fade and scroll.
- **Smooth edges of screen fonts.** Makes text easier to read.
- **Use large icons.** Makes icons easier to see.
- **Show icons using all possible colors.** Creates a more attractive appearance.
- **Show window contents while dragging.** Ensures that the contents of windows are always visible when being moved around the screen.
- **Hide keyboard navigation indicators until I use the Alt key.** Hides the underlined characters in menus and controls. These underlined characters indicate shortcut keys during normal operation.

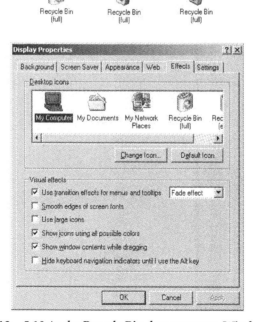

Figure 5.12—5.13 As the Recycle Bin demonstrates, Windows 2000
lets you choose from a wide range of special effects

Each of these visual effects creates a small performance hit on your computer's resources but enabling them usually produces a negligible effect leaving their selection as a matter of personal preference.

Note: *In order to use the Smooth edges of screen fonts options, your computer's video card must support a minimum of 256 colors.*

Changing Settings

Color depth and resolution, managed by the Settings property sheet shown in Figure 5.14, are two of the most important visual elements. Color depth determines how realistic and attractive your display will be. The Resolution setting controls the size of your desktop and the size of everything that appears on it.

The available depth of colors and range of supported resolutions depends upon your computer video adapter card. More expensive cards with more on-board memory will support a larger range of options. Typical color schemes include:

- **16 Colors.** A minimum color setting which provides relatively low quality graphics support.
- **256 colors.** A moderate color range capable of displaying fairly realistic graphic images.
- **High Color (16 bit).** A range of over 65,000 colors that provides realistic visual effects.
- **True Color (32 bit).** A range of over 16 million colors providing excellent visual effects.

To set color depth, select a color setting from the Colors drop-down list and click on OK. To change resolution, use your mouse to drag the slider bar to the right or left and click on OK.

Tip!   Enabling a color depth or resolution that your monitor does not support will corrupt your display and render it un-viewable. After making the display changes, Windows 2000 requires you to confirm that you are happy with the changes. Windows 2000 first gives you 15 seconds to change you mind after changing display settings. If after making changes you are unable to view your display, just sit tight, and Windows 2000 will undo the changes when you fail to respond to this confirmation prompt.

The Advanced button allows you to configure advanced settings including whether or not you must restart your computer before the new display changes are applied. By default Windows 2000 applies new display settings without restarting your computer. Some older programs do not behave properly if you make display changes this way, and as a result, you may end up having to restart your computer anyway.

The other two options of this property sheet are Troubleshoot and Advanced. The Troubleshoot button starts the Display Troubleshooter shown in Figure 5.15. This troubleshooter will ask you a series of questions and can help you to solve most of the problems you might come across when making changes to your display.

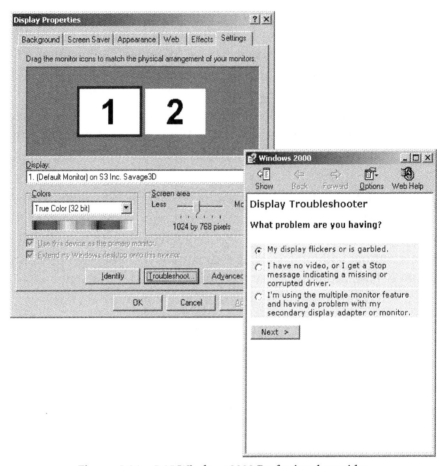

Figures 5.14—5.15 Windows 2000 Professional provides
a wide range of configuration options and helps you to solve
any display problems that may arise should you
make a configuration mistake

Using Multiple Monitors

One of the coolest new features in Windows 2000 Professional is its
support for multiple monitors. If you have the proper hardware, you
can now attach as many as 9 monitors to your computer and spread

your desktop over them. This means you can do things like work with a different application on each monitor. You will find this is much easier than having to constantly switch between multiple applications on a single monitor.

No matter how many monitors you hook up, one will always be the primary monitor. This is where all BIOS messages will appear during system starts up and where most of your applications will open when you start them.

Note: *Any games that you have will probably be limited to using the primary monitor unless the software vendor has written them to take advantage of this new feature.*

Requirements

The multiple monitor feature only works with PCI and AGP video cards. So if you have a computer that only accepts older VLB, ISA, EISA cards, you will not be able to take advantage of this feature. If your computer is not too old it may have an AGP video card. *AGP* stands for *Advanced Graphics Accelerator* and represents the state of the art in video card technology. Computers today are limited to a single AGP video card slot so any additional video cards would have to be PCI cards. So whether you already have a PCI or AGP video card, any additional cards must be PCI. In addition, your extra video cards will need a multiple monitor software driver.

Note: *Be careful when purchasing additional video cards. While just about any PCI or AGP video card can serve as your primary display, the remaining video cards must come with multiple display software drivers. As of the writing of this book finding such cards is difficult. Because of its popularity AGP is quickly becoming the new standard for video cards which means it is getting harder to find PCI cards. And the only PCI cards that currently have multiple monitor software drivers are the high-end video cards. Always be sure to check with the video card manufacturer to make sure that they provide Windows 2000 compatible drivers and that the cards driver supports the multiple monitor feature before making your purchase.*

Note: *If you're not experienced in installing computer hardware, it is best to have a trained technician install your second video card. In many cases installing your own hardware can invalidate your computer's warranty.*

Installing additional monitors

The following procedure outlines the steps involved in installing a second video card:

1. Power off your computer and remove its case.

2. Insert your PCI video card into an open expansion slot and replace the computer's case.

3. Power on the computer. Windows 2000 Professional should automatically detect and install the new video card.

4. Open the Display Properties dialog and click on the Settings property sheet and make sure that your new video card and monitor appear.

Tip!   *If your new video card and monitor do not appear on the Display Properties dialog, start the Device Manger and look for clues as to why the card is not working. If the Device manager does not show the new video card either, try using the Add New Hardware utility in the Windows 2000 Control Panel to install it.*

Which video card is made the primary card depends upon several factors none of which are controlled by Windows 2000. Depending on your computer's *BIOS* your computer may default to either AGP or PCI. Check with the manufacturer, you may be able to change this. If all you have is PCI slots then the primary card is determined based on the order in which BIOS initializes the PCI slots. You can always swap your PCI cards around in order to set a specific one up as the primary card.

If you are unable to determine which monitor is which when looking at the Settings property sheet, you can right-click on each monitor and select Identify. Windows 2000 will then display a large number on top of both the monitor and the graphic that represents it. Figure 5.16 shows how this might look on your computer. This should make it easy for you to configure your multiple monitor set up.

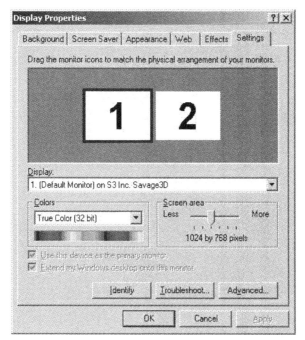

**Figure 5.16 Multiple monitor support is a new technology
that allows you to spread your desktop over two or more monitors**

Tip!   *You do not have to purchase additional video cards to take advantage of multiple monitors. Video card manufacturers are beginning to come out with multiple port video adapter cards which can connect 2 or more monitors to your computer. Of course, these cards are many times more expensive than their single port counterparts. Hopefully the cost of these new cards will come down over time.*

Note: *If your computer's motherboard has an on-board graphics port you may not be able to use it in a multiple monitor scenario. In this case you would need to supply video cards.*

Each monitor will display its own desktop background. But only one monitor, that you can select, will contain the Windows 2000 Taskbar. After starting an application you can drag it from the primary monitor to any other monitor.

How you drag and drop applications depends on how you have configured your multiple monitor layout. This is performed using the Display Properties dialog. For example, Figures 5.17—5.19 show three different configurations using two monitors. The actual number of possible configurations is endless.

Figures 5.17—5.19 Windows 2000 Professional's multiple
monitor support allows for an unlimited number of configurations
including horizontal, vertical and diagonal

Note: *Not all screen savers will support multiple monitors. Check with the software vendors who create them. However, all the screen savers shipped on the Windows 2000 Professional CD support this feature.*

CHAPTER 6

Working With Your Applications

Windows 2000 Professional provides a collection of free applications that are automatically installed during the installation of the operating system. The applications can be found by clicking on Start, Programs and the Accessories. They include a word processor, paint program, multi media applications and a collection of games.

The applications provided with Windows 2000 Professional provide a good starter set but there are much better applications on the market that provide a host of additional features. For example, word processing applications such as Microsoft Word provide features way beyond the basic set you get with Windows 2000 Professional's WordPad application. To take advantage of other applications you need to know how to install and work with them. This chapter will provide you with the information you need to install and manage your applications.

Microsoft Windows Logo

No matter how good Windows 2000 Professional may be as an operating system, ultimately your computer is only as good as the applications you run on it. If you have ever downloaded a freeware or shareware program from the Internet that its author released before its time, then you know what I mean. To help ensure the integrity of your system, look for applications that display the *Microsoft Windows Logo*.

In order to get this logo on their product, software vendors must ensure their programs meet the *Microsoft Application Specification* for Windows 2000. This specification is a set of requirements Microsoft has created that specifies the qualities a reliable Windows application should have. For example, qualified applications should work with the Windows Installer Service and work properly when upgraded from another Windows operating system. VeriTest, an independent testing laboratory, has tested all logo-bearing applications.

Tip!   *Just because you purchase a piece of software that contains the Microsoft Windows Logo does not meant the applications will do what you want it to do or that it is a good program. The logo only guarantees the applications that passed all compliance tests. There is no substitute for researching applications and making sure you know what you are buying.*

Windows Installer Service

The *Windows Installer Service* is a new feature introduced by Windows 2000. It's not something you work with directly, but it does a lot for you and knowing a little about it can help increase your familiarity with Windows 2000. The basic function of this service it to manage the life cycle of your applications. It manages the installation and removal of Windows applications and monitors them to ensure their integrity.

Applications designed to work with this service register their components during installation. If at some point a key file for one of your applications gets corrupted or accidentally deleted, the Windows Installer Service will automatically try to repair or replace it. So while you may not see it, the Windows Installer Service does a lot for you.

Note: *Any application you install that does not have the Windows logo may not work with the Windows Installer Service. This means, should problems occur, it might be up to you to fix them.*

Using The Add/Remove Programs utility

The *Add/Remove Programs* utility is located in the Windows 2000 Control Panel. It acts as an intermediary between you and the Windows Installer Service. It provides three services:

- Change or Remove Programs
- Add New Programs
- Add/Remove Windows Components

You will use this utility to install and manage not only your applications but also with any Windows component software that you did not install during the initial installation of Windows 2000 Professional.

Changing And Removing Programs

This options lets you view and manage all currently installed applications as shown in Figure 6.1. In addition to listing all registered applications, you can get more detail information about a specific application by selecting it.

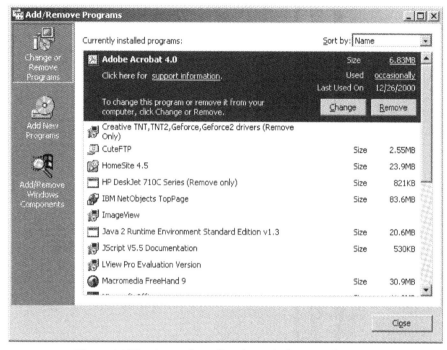

Figure 6.1 Viewing and configuring Windows applications

The information provided includes:

* How much hard disk space the application uses
* How often you use the application
* The last time the application was used

Each application will also have either a Change/Remove button or a Change and a Remove button. Clicking on Change/Remove generally starts the uninstall process for the application. If the application has a separate Change and Remove button, the Remove button starts the uninstall process and the Change button typically allows you to install other pieces of the application. For example, you might have installed

Microsoft Office but elected to put off the installation of the Microsoft Excel until a later date.

In the upper right hand corner is a Sort By option which allows you to sort your applications list by any of the following criteria:

- Name
- Size
- Frequency Of Use
- Date Last Used

Adding New Programs

The Add New Programs option assists you in installing new applications as shown in Figure 6.2.

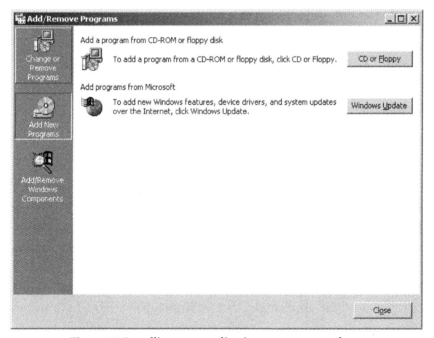

Figure 6.2 Installing new applications or system updates

Two options are available:

- **Add a program from CD-ROM or floppy disk.** This is where you install your applications. Simply insert the media containing the application into the appropriate drive and click on the CD or Floppy button. Windows 2000 will look in both places to find your application. If it does not find one it will ask you to tell it where it is. This allows you the opportunity to browse and install applications that may reside on a network connection.

- **Add programs from Microsoft.** This option requires an Internet connection and allows you to gather and install the latest features, drivers, fixes, and service packs directly from the Microsoft Windows 2000 Update web site. Simply click on the Windows Update button and it contacts the web site and performs an analysis of your computer to determine which of the available software downloads is appropriate for your configuration.

Managing Windows Components

This option starts the *Windows Components Wizard*, shown in Figure 6.3, which allows you to go back and install Windows components you did not chose to install when you upgraded to Windows 2000. You can also uninstall any components you no longer need. To install a new component select it from the list and click on Next. To remove a component clear it's selection and click on Next.

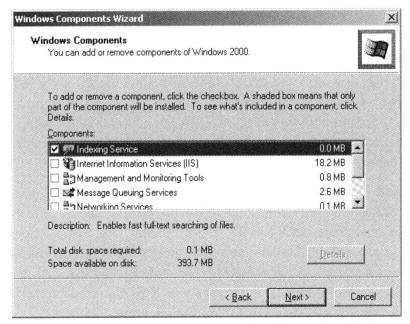

Figure 6.3 The Windows Components wizard lets you install and remove optional Windows 2000 Professional software components

Note: *Depending on the component which you installed some additional configuration may be required before the component can be used. Consult the Windows 2000 help system for information on configuring individual components.*

Installing Via The Windows 2000 Desktop

Of course, you can still install your Windows applications in the more traditional ways. If your application comes on a CD then it will probably automatically launch its installation the first time that you put the CD in the CD-ROM drive. Go ahead and follow the instruction on the screen and allow the installation to continue. As long as the applications displayed the Windows Logo it should go ahead and register itself with the Windows Installer Service.

If your application is on a floppy disk then you can begin its installation by double-clicking on its setup program from Windows Explorer or the My Computer dialogs. You can also install the application by clicking on Start and then Run and typing in the location of its setup program which should be provided in the application's documentation.

Launching Applications

Some applications offer to create a shortcut on the Windows desktop that you can double-click on to start the application. Other applications may place an icon on the Quick Launch Toolbar or the System Tray.

Regardless of whether your applications do this or not, you can always find them on the Programs menu. Even if you are installing older Windows applications, Windows 2000 Professional will create a folder for the application and place it under the Programs menu. All that you have to do is click on Start, Programs, and the folder that contains the application and then on the application itself.

Tip!   *For added convenience you can place application shortcuts on the top of the Start menu by dragging and dropping them onto the Start button on the Taskbar.*

Working With Applications

Because there are so many Windows applications and each has its own unique features, it is not possible to explain how each one works. However, Windows applications do possess a common set of standards, which means that once you have mastered one application you will already know much of what you need to work with another one. This section will attempt to outline and explain most of these commonalties using the WordPad application as an example. WordPad, shown in Figure 6.4, is one of the free applications that ships with Windows 2000 Professional. It is started by clicking on Start, Programs, Accessories and then WordPad.

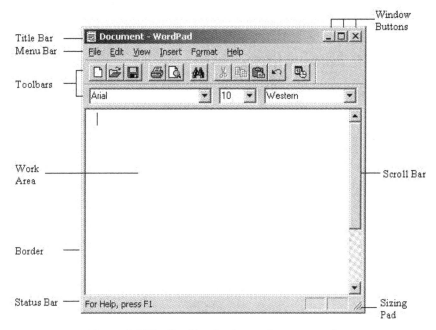

Figure 6.4 WordPad is a basic word processor that comes with Windows 2000 Professional

The following components comprise the WordPad application:

- **Title Bar**—Identifies the application in use and the name of the currently open document.
- **Menu Bar**—Contains menus that provide easy access to commonly used commands.

- **Toolbars**—Contains icons that provide access to many of the commonly used commands found on the Menu Bar. Applications often have more than one toolbar.
- **Work Area**—The portion of the application where you work. In the case of WordPad it is where you type your document.
- **Border**—A thin area that identifies the sides of the application.
- **Status Bar**—The area at the bottom of the application where application status messages are displayed.
- **Windows Buttons**—Small buttons in the upper right-hand corner of the application that allow you to minimize, maximize and terminate the application.
- **Scroll Bar**—A bar that appears on the bottom and or the right hand side of the application as needed to help you navigate your document by dragging the bar from one end to the other.
- **Sizing Pad**—An area in the bottom right hand corner of the application that you can use to change the size of the application using drag and drop.

Saving And Retrieving Your Work

Regardless of what applications you run and which commands you execute when using them, you will need to save and to able to retrieve your work. These tasks are performed from the *Open* and *Save As* dialogs shown in Figure 6.5 and 6.6. If you have ever worked with a windows operating system before such as Windows NT or Windows 95, you are going to appreciate the improvements that Microsoft has made to these dialogs. Working with files is much easier and faster. By default these dialogs will look in the My Documents folder making it easy to retrieve your personal work. On the left side of the dialog are 5 shortcuts that link to the places where you will most likely need to go to find your documents. These include the following links:

- **History**. Provides access to files that you have worked with in the past.

- **Desktop.** Provides quick access to any files or shortcuts to files that are stored directly on you desktop.
- **My Documents.** The default location for all your work.
- **My Computer.** Provides access to all the drives on your computer as well as network drive mappings you may have created.
- **My Network Places.** Your starting point for finding network resources. It contains any Network Places which you may have configured and allows you to browse the network.

If you prefer you can click on the arrow for the Look in field at the top of the dialog and specify the location where the file resides and then drill down to find it. Just to the right of the Look in field are 4 icons that provide the following options:

- **Go to last folder visited.** Opens the folder you last accessed.
- **Up one level.** Opens the next high-level folder. For example, if you are in a folder it opens its parent folder, and if you are in My Computer, it opens the Desktop.
- **Create new folder.** Lets you create new folders making it easy for you to organize your files.
- **View menu.** Lets you choose from any of 5 views that control how your files and subfolders appear. These views include large icons, small icons, lists, details and thumbnails.

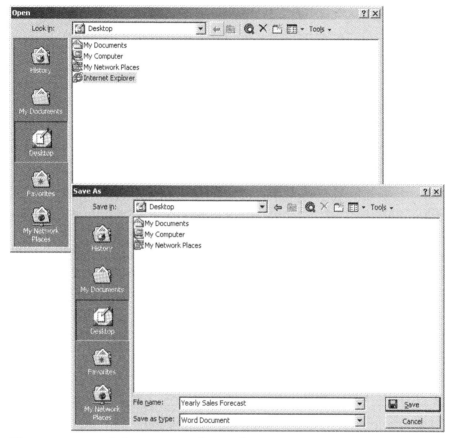

Figures 6.5—6.6 Windows 2000 Professional's Open and Save As dialogs provides a range of options that assist you in the process of storing and retrieving your files

Each Windows application shares a common look and feel. However, no two applications are exactly the same and the only way to really learn how they operate is to start them up and begin working with them.

Switching Between Active Applications

One of the really great things about Windows is its ability to *multitask* between multiple applications. This means you can easily work with several of your applications at the same time and switch between them as necessary. One way to do this is to click on the *Minimize* button in the upper right hand corner of the application every time you want to move it out of the way.

Clicking on the minimize button removes the application from the desktop without closing it. The application is still visible on the taskbar at the bottom of the page. You can begin working with the application again by clicking on the application in the taskbar. This will restore the application to its previous size and location. If the application is not taking up the entire display area, you can increase its size by clicking on the Maximize button. This changes the maximize button to the *Restore* button, which if you click it restores the application to its previous size and location. If you are finished working with an application, you can close it by using the Menu bar or by clicking on the *Close* button. If you have any unsaved work, Windows 2000 Professional will prompt you to save it before terminating the application.

Another way that you can manage an application is by right clicking on its title bar or on the icon that represents it on the Windows 2000 Professional Taskbar and select the appropriate option from the popup menu that appears.

Using The Task Manager To Control Applications

The Applications property sheet on the Windows *Task Manager* provides another means for managing your applications. The Task Manager is started by either right clicking on an open area on the Windows 2000 Professional Task Bar and selecting T̲ask Manager or by simultaneously holding down the CTRL+ALT+DEL keys and selecting the Task Manager button on the Windows Security dialog when it appears. The Applications property sheet is selected by default as shown in Figure 6.7.

Figure 6.7 The Windows 2000 Task Manager provides information about all active applications and allows you to terminate applications that have stopped responding

Every active application will be listed and its status displayed. Possible status options include Running and Not Responding. An application listed as Not Responding may have experienced an error and become unresponsive preventing you from either working with it or terminating it. In that case you can terminate the application by selecting it and clicking on End Task. Windows 2000 Professional will prompt you for confirmation before terminating the application.

Note: *Be very careful when terminating applications using the Task Manager because you will loose any unsaved work.*

You can begin working with any active application by selecting it and clicking on the Switch To button. Clicking on the New Task button opens the Create New Task dialog, which provides a quick way to open an application by allowing you to type in its name.

CHAPTER 7

Basic Administrative Tasks

Up until now this book has focused exclusively on providing you with instruction on the types of things that are important to Windows 2000 Professional users and has avoided issues dealing with advanced administrative tasks. Administrative tasks are typically the responsibility of network or system administrators, and chances are good that if your computer is connected to a network, you will not be authorized to perform most administrative tasks anyway, including some of the tasks found in this chapter. However, an understanding of how to perform these tasks can provide valuable insight into how things work on your computer.

If you are working on your own personal computer at home or on a computer at work where you are permitted to perform some of your own administrative tasks, then this chapter will provide you with instruction on how to perform three common administrative tasks. These include:

- Setting up a printer
- Performing basic user account maintenance
- Getting connected to the Internet

Installing A Printer

Like just about everything in Windows 2000 Professional, printers are added and configured using a Wizard. The Add Printer wizard guides you through the process of setting up either a local or a network printer. A *local printer* is a print device connected to your computer's parallel port, and a *network printer* is one that a network administrator has setup to be shared over a computer network. This chapter will demonstrate how to install and test a local printer although the steps to install a network printer are very similar.

If you are unable to attach your printer at this time, you can still complete this process and attach the printer at a later date. The benefit to having the printer setup and ready to go is you can print a test page when you are done that verifies a successful installation. So if you know what type of printer you will be installing, you can go ahead and perform this procedure and everything will be setup and ready to go when you finally hook up your printer.

Note: *If your printer is relatively new, then it may support plug and play installation. If this is the case, then Windows 2000 Professional should be able to detect your printer and install it. After you attach your printer and power your computer on, you may be asked to supply the diskette or CD that came with the printer.*

The process of installing a local printer begins by starting the Add Printer Wizard and answering a few questions as demonstrated below:

1. Attach your printer to your computer's parallel printer port and power it on.
2. Click on Start, Settings, Printers and then Add Printer.
3. The Add Printer Wizard dialog appears. Click on **Next**.
4. You are prompted to perform either a local printer installation or a network installation as shown in Figure 7.1. Select **Local printer**. If your printer is plug and play compatible select the **Automatically detect and install my Plug and Play printer** and

follow the instructions that are presented. Otherwise leave that option cleared and click on **N**ext.

5. You are asked to specify the port where the printer has been connected as shown in Figure 7.2. All computers come with a standard parallel port that Windows will identify as LPT1. Select **U**se the following port and then choose the LPT1 option and click on **N**ext.

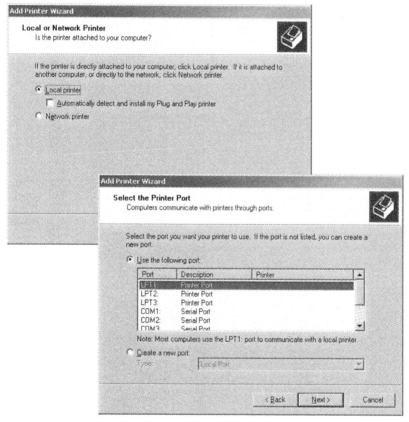

Figures 7.1—72. Selecting the port that will be used to set up the local printer

6. Select the manufacturer's name of your printer from the **M**anufacturers list and pick the appropriate model from the **P**rinters

list as shown in Figure 7.3 and click **Next**. If you do not see the printer manufacturer's name or the correct model of your printer, then click on **Have Disk,** and when prompted insert the diskette or CD that came with your printer and follow the instructions presented.

7. Windows 2000 Professional supplies a default name for the printer as shown in Figure 7.4. If you like, you may change this name before clicking on **Next**.

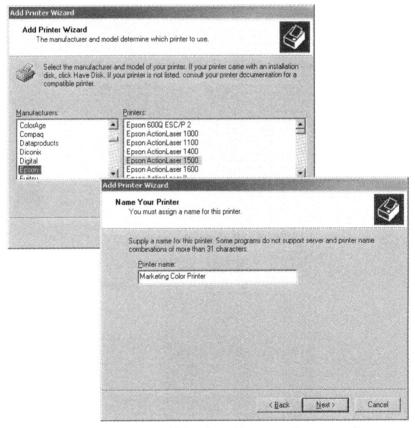

Figures 7.3—7.4 Specifying the printer manufacturer and model and assigning a friendly printer name

8. If your computer is on a network, Windows 2000 Professional will ask you if you wish to share you computer with other network users as shown in Figure 7.5. This will allow your co-workers to setup the printer on their own computer and send print jobs to it. Unless you have been given permission to do this, you should select **Do not share this printer** and click on **N**ext.

9. The last thing Windows 2000 Professional does is asks you if you want to print a test page as shown in Figure 7.6. This is the fastest and easiest way to verify you have successfully installed the printer. Click **Y**es to perform the test. If you do not want to perform the test or if you have not attached your printer yet, click on **N**o. Click **N**ext.

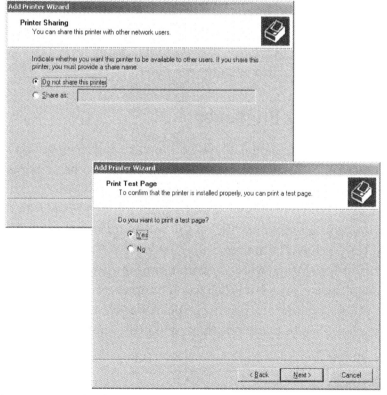

Figure 7.5—7.6 Finishing up the printer installation and printing a test page

10. Windows 2000 Professional displays a summary of all the information you have provided to the Add Printer Wizard. Review the information, and if everything is correct, click on **Finish**.
11. Windows 2000 Professional will now install your printer. When done it will print a test page if you instructed it to do so. Click on **OK** if everything works as expected. Otherwise click on **Troubleshoot** and follow the instructions as presented.

Your printer is now installed and ready to print. If you look in the Printers folder you will see that Windows 2000 Professional has created a new icon representing your printer.

Tip!   *Try and give a descriptive name to your printer. For example, you might include its model number, your name or a description of its color capabilities. This will make things clearer for anyone else who might need to work with the computer.*

Managing Your Print Jobs

Windows 2000 Professional allows you to view and manage your print jobs on a printer-by-printer basis. So if you had two printers installed on your computer, you would manage the print jobs you send to each printer separately. When you submit a print job to a printer it actually gets spooled as a temporary file on the computer's hard drive. Jobs are spooled and printed in the order they are received. If there are no print jobs currently printing, windows will submit the print job immediately. As soon as the job prints, it is deleted. If another job is already printing, the print job waits for its turn in the print queue. A *print queue* is simply a managed list of print jobs waiting to print on the printer.

There are several management tasks that you can perform when working with your print jobs. These tasks are outlined below:

- Pause an individual print job or the entire print queue
- Resume the printing of a paused job or all jobs in a paused print queue. A paused job begins printing at the point where is was paused
- Restart the printing of a paused job or all jobs in a paused print queue from the beginning
- Cancel a print job or purge all print jobs in the a print queue

There are several reasons you might need to manage your print jobs. For example, you may have accidentally submitted the wrong print job and want to delete it before it prints or you may notice that your printer is beginning to exhaust its ink or toner supply right in the middle of a large print job. After pausing the job you can replenish the ink or toner supply and then resume the print job thus saving you the hassle of having to reprint the job all over again.

Figure 7.7 shows the Windows 2000 Professional print queue for a printer named Marketing Color Printer. In this example there is one print job currently printing and two more are spooled and waiting to be submitted to the printer.

Managing Individual Print Jobs

You can manage individual print jobs using the menu commands available under the Document menu as demonstrated in Figure 7.8. The available options are:

- **Pause**—Pauses the printing of the currently selected print job
- **Resume**—Begins printing a currently paused print job at the point where it was when the print job was paused
- **Restart**—Starts a paused print job over from the beginning
- **Cancel**—Deletes a print job

- **Properties**—Provides information about the print job including its size, number of copies, and resolution.

To execute one of these options select a print job and then choose one of the commands.

Note: *If you cancel a job that is in the process of printing, Windows 2000 Professional will stop submitting the job to the printer and will delete the print job from the print queue. However, any part of the print job that has already been submitted to the printer will continue printing.*

Managing A Print Queue

Instead of managing individual print jobs you may need to manage all the print jobs in a print queue at the same time. There are two commands available under the Printer menu for managing the entire print queue. The commands are outline below:

- **Pause Printing**—Pauses the printing of the current print job and prevents any further jobs from being submitted
- **Cancel All Documents**—Deletes all print jobs in the print queue

Figure 7.9 shows an example of a print queue where all printing has been paused. The check mark to the left of the Pause Printing command shows the option has been selected. To resume the printing of print jobs in the queue, simply select the Pause Printing command again. The check mark will disappear and printing will resume.

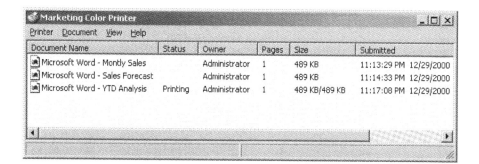

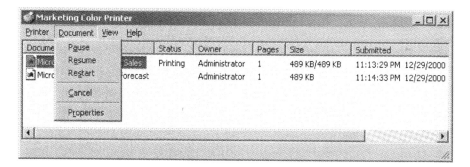

Figures 7.7—7.9 Double-clicking on a printer's icon shows the contents of its print queue and allows you to manage all of your print jobs

Administering User Accounts

You need a user account and password to log on and use a Windows 2000 Professional. Administering Windows 2000 security is a complicated topic that by itself can easily fill up an entire book. It involves the creation and management of user accounts and security permissions as well as the establishment of security policies. This section will limit its focus to the creation of user accounts that are required for logging in.

Guest, User and Administrator Accounts

When Windows 2000 Professional is installed on a new computer three user accounts are created. One is the *Guest* account, which provides the ability to log on to the computer and open applications and save documents. This account is unable to install any software programs or make configuration changes to the computer.

Another account that is created is the *Administrator* account. This account is the most powerful account on the computer. It has complete access to all resources on the computer and can be used to perform any task.

The last account created during installation is a normal user account. This is the account you should be using during the normal operation of your computer. It allows you to make modifications to the computer and to install new software programs but prevents you from accessing any files on the computer that might belong to somebody else.

If your computer is part of a company network you may find you are prevented from performing any account administration on your computer because this responsibility has been assigned to a network administration group. However, if this is not the case or if this is your own personal computer and you need to share it with other co-workers or family members, you will need to know how to create and manage additional user accounts.

The easiest way to administer user accounts on a Windows 2000 Professional computer is with the User and Passwords utility that is located in the Windows 2000 Professional Control Panel. Figure 7.10 shows how the Users and Password utility looks when accessed for the first time. This utility consist of two property sheets although the Users property sheet is the only one you will need to use when managing user accounts on an individual Windows 2000 Professional computer.

Establishing An Automatic Log In

At the top of the Users property sheet you will see the Users must enter a user name and password to use this computer option. This option is enabled by default and prevents anyone from using the computer without first logging in with a valid account name and password. If you disable this option and click on OK you will be prompted to provide a default account name and password that will be used to automatically log in to Windows 2000 Professional every time the computer is started. This option can be very convenient but it makes your computer available to anyone who has physical access to it and should be implemented with caution.

Working With User Accounts

As you can see in Figure 7.10, there are three user accounts that have been defined. Just beneath the list of existing user accounts are three buttons labeled Add, Remove and Properties. Clicking on the Add button starts the Add New User wizard which steps you through the process of creating a new user account. Selecting a user account and then clicking on the Remove button tells Windows 2000 Professional to delete the account. Selecting an account and the clicking on the Properties button lets you make changes to the account.

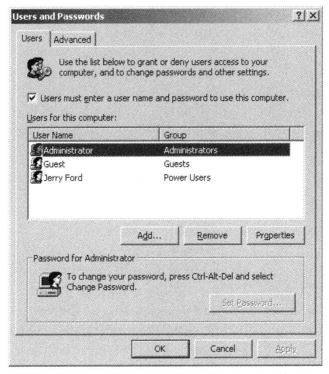

Figure 7.10 The Users and Password dialog allows you to administer user
accounts and passwords on your local computer

The process of creating an account is very straight forward as outlined
below:

1. Click on the **Ad̲d** button on the Users and Passwords utility. The
   Add New User Wizard appears as shown in Figure 7.11.

2. Type the name of the user account you are going to create and
   type in the user's name and optionally provide description
   information and then click on **N̲ext**.

3. Assign a password to the account by typing it in to the **P**assword field. Type the password a second time the **C**onfirm **Password** field as demonstrated in Figure 7.12 and then click on **N**ext.

4. Select the appropriate level of access to assign to the user account as demonstrated in Figure 7.13. The default is **S**tandard **User,** which allows the user to install programs and customize their working environment without allowing access to files that belong to other users. **R**estricted user permits logging in and working but prevents the user from making any major environmental changes such as installing new programs or making configuration changes to the computer. **O**ther lets you select and assign more specialized roles to the user account. The available selections for this option include:

 - **Administrators**—Have complete access to system resources
 - **Backup Operators**—Are authorized to run the backup programs and backup all files and folders on the computer
 - **Guests**—Limited to creating and saving documents
 - **Power Users**—Can make modifications to the computer and install software applications but cannot access other users' files
 - **Replicator**—A special purpose group used by the operating system which is not appropriate for individual user accounts
 - **Users**—Can create and save documents but have limited ability to make changes to the computer

Click on **Finish** after specifying the appropriate level of account access. The new user account will appear in the list of user accounts on the Users and Passwords dialog.

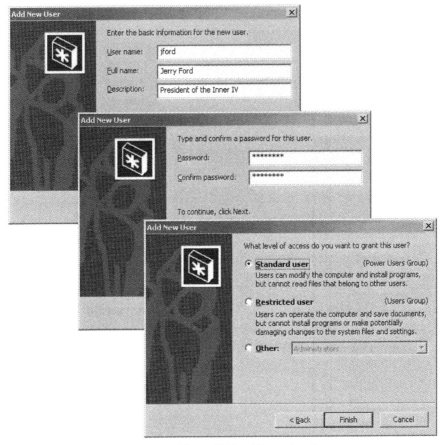

Figures 7.11—7.13 The Add New User wizard steps you
through the process of creating a new user account

Resetting User Account Passwords

From time to time users may forget their passwords and therefore will
not be unable to log in to the computer. When this occurs they will need
someone with administrative privileges to reset their password.

Use the following procedure to unlock a user's account:

1. Log in to the computer using either the Administrator account or a user account that was assigned administrative access privileges and then start the User and Passwords utility.

2. Select the user account that has been locked out and click on Set Password. The Set Password dialog appears.

3. Type a new password in the New password and Confirm new password fields and click on OK.

4. Notify the user and tell him or her what their new password is.

Connecting To The Internet

One of the major benefits of owning a personal computer is the ability to access the Internet and the infinite amount of information and fun it provides. Windows 2000 Professional supplies all the software you will need. The only thing you will need to supply is the hardware to get connected. The most common way for home user to get connected is via a modem and a telephone line. If your computer is connected to a network you may be able to connect to the Internet over your network. Check with your network administrator to see if this option is available to you. The remainder of this chapter will focus on showing you how to install a modem and get connected.

Note: *Cable modems are becoming more popular and provide faster access to the Internet. You can call your local cable company to find out if that option is available. If it is your cable company will usually come out to your house or business and set up everything for you as a part of the service.*

There are three basic steps to setting up Internet access using a modem. The first step is to install the modem and attach it to a telephone line. There are two types of modems: internal and external. An external modem is attached to a serial port on the back of your computer while an internal modem is inserted into an open expansion slot on the motherboard inside your computer. While installing an external modem is a relatively simple task, installing an internal modem is a bit more complicated because you have to get into the interior of your computer. A discussion of how to physically install hardware is beyond the scope of this book, and it is advised that you have someone who is familiar with working on computer hardware do the installation for you. Once your modem is installed remember to attach it to a phone line, and you are ready to perform the software portion of the installation.

Installing A Modem

As long as your modem is not too old, Windows 2000 Professional should automatically see it and install it when you startup your computer. After physically installing it you may be asked to supply the diskette or CD that came with the modem. The following procedure outlines how to install your modem when Windows 2000 Professional does not plug and play install it for you.

The software portion of the modem installation process can be performed on the Phone and Modem Options utility located in the Windows 2000 Professional Control Panel and is outlined below:

1. Open the Phone and Modem Option dialog located in the Windows 2000 Professional Control Panel. A Location Information dialog will appear asking you to specify the location of the computer. Fill in this dialog with the country and area code. Provide the remaining information as required and click on **OK**.

2. The Phone and Modem Options dialog will now display an entry representing the information you just provided. Select the Modems property sheet and click on **Ad̲d**.

3. Select **D̲on't detect my modem; I will select it from a list** as shown in Figure 7.14 and click on **N̲ext**.

4. Select the modem's manufacturer and model from the list that appears as shown in Figure 7.15. If you do not see matching entries, click on **Have Disk** and supply the diskette or CD that came with the modem when prompted. Click on **N̲ext**.

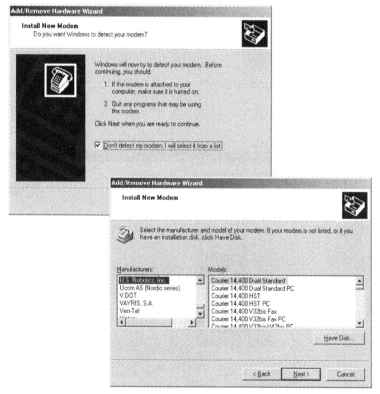

Figures 7.14—7.15 Performing a manual install
by selecting the modem manufacturer and model

5. Windows 2000 displays the name of the modem you have just selected as shown in Figure 7.16. Verify this information is correct and click on Next.

6. Select a port from the list of available ports as shown in Figure 7.17. If this is an external modem, the port number coincides with the serial port number when the modem is attached. Click on Next.

Figures 7.16—7.17 Verifying modem information
and assigning a communications port

Windows will now install your modem. Windows will notify you when it is done. Click on **Finish**. An entry for the modem will now appear in the Phone and Modem Options dialog.

Note: *If you received a message that says Windows cannot find a digital signature for your modem, you can continue with the installation by clicking on Yes. With Windows 2000 Microsoft has begun providing digital signatures for software that accompany peripheral devices. This digital signature means the software has been tested and approved by Microsoft. The fact you received this message means the software on your modem's diskette or CD is unsigned. You may be able to download a newer version of the software from the modem manufacturer's web site. However, your modem will probably work perfectly well without a digital signature.*

Connecting To The World Wide Web

Now that you have a properly installed modem you are ready to create your connection to the Internet. Windows 2000 Professional provides the Internet Connection Wizard, shown in Figure 7.18, to help step you through this process. You can start it by selecting Start, Programs, Accessories, Communications and the Internet Connection Wizard.

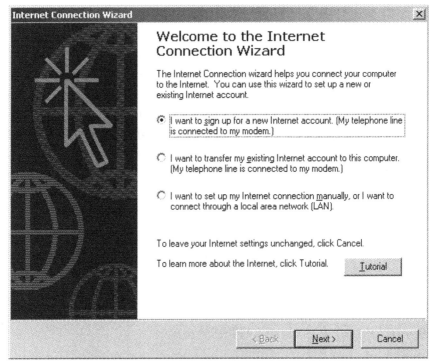

Figure 7.18 The Internet Connection Wizard will guide you
through the process of setting up your Internet connection

If you have never been on the Internet before and do not have an
Internet account select, I want to sign up for a new Internet account.
This option will help you to find and sign up with an Internet Service
provider. If you already have an Internet account setup, then you should
select I want to transfer my existing Internet account to this computer.
This option steps you through the process of getting everything set up
under Windows 2000 Professional. The third option provided by the
Internet Connection Wizard is for experienced users or users whose
computer is connected to a network where the network administrator
has set up shared Internet access. Consult with your network administrator before using this option.

Once you have everything set up and have connected to an Internet service provider, you are ready to surf the World Wide Wide. If you have not already done so, start Internet Explorer and start surfing.

About the Author

Jerry Lee Ford, Jr. is an author, educator and IT professional with over 13 years experience in the information technology field. He holds a Masters in Business Administration from Virginia Commonwealth University in Richmond, Virginia. Jerry is a Microsoft Certified Systems Engineer and the author of several other books including *Practical Microsoft Windows Peer Networking, Upgrading to Windows 2000 Professional* and *Learn JavaScript in a Weekend.* He has over five years experience as an adjunct instructor teaching networking courses in Information Technology. He lives in Hanover, Virginia with his wife, Mary, and their sons, Alexander and William.

Glossary

Accelerated Graphics Port (AGP). A state of the art advanced video card that provides for the movement of large amounts of 3D data between the video adapter card and the computer's memory system.

Accessories. A folder located off of the Programs menu that contains collections of bundled software that comes with Windows 2000 Professional.

Active Desktop. A feature of Windows 2000 that allows you to place live web content directly on your desktop that is automatically updated as long as access to the Internet is available.

Active Desktop Gallery. A Microsoft web site that provides free active desktop content.

Add/Remove Hardware. A Windows 2000 utility that assists in the installation and removal of computer peripheral devices.

Administrator. The most powerful computer account on a Windows 2000 system with access to all system resources.

Advanced Power Management. A feature built into Windows 2000 that allows it to take control of power allocation to system resources.

Application. A software program such as Microsoft Word that performs one of more tasks.

AutoComplete. A feature added to Windows dialogs that attempts to complete fields based on the text that you have typed so far.

AutoCorrect. Automatically corrects typographical errors as you type in Windows dialogs.

Automatic Proxy Configuration. The ability of a Windows 2000 computer to automatically discover and configure itself to use a network proxy server in order to gain access to the Internet.

BIOS. A collection of software routines that test computer hardware during system startup before finding and loading the operating system.

Boot.ini. A system file used to boot Windows 2000.

Boot Menu. A menu of Windows 2000 boot options that are defined in the boot.ini file.

Control Panel. A Windows folder that contains a collection of configuration utilities.

Data Encryption. The process of encoding data that only its creator can decode to access its contents.

Desktop. The screen that appears after logging into Windows 2000. It can contain both active contents and shortcuts.

Direct Connection. A connection established between two computers using either a parallel, serial or infrared connection.

Disk Quotas. The ability to establish a predetermined limit on the amount of space that users can consume on a local disk drive.

Domain. An organizational construct used by large Microsoft Windows networks for grouping, managing and securing computer resources on a network.

Dual-boot. The ability to start a computer and select from 2 or more operating systems.

DVD. A disk storage technology that uses digital video disc technology and can access CD and DVD media.

Encrypted File System. Adds additional security to Windows 2000 computers by providing for the storage of encrypted information on drives, folders and files on NTFS formatted drives.

FAT. A non-secure 16-bit file system that is supported by all Microsoft operating systems.

FAT32. A non-secure 32-bit file system introduced by Windows 98 but supported on Windows 2000.

File. A collection of data such as a Microsoft Word document or a graphic image.

Folder. A container that contains collections of files, applications and even other folders.

Guest. A user account that provides the ability to log on, open applications and save documents.

Hardware Compatibility List (HCL). A list maintained by Microsoft at their web site that identifies all hardware that has been tested on Windows 2000.

Hibernation. The ability to save your current working environment before powering down a Windows 2000 computer and have it automatically restored upon startup.

Hot Docking. The ability to remove a portable computer from its docking bay without first powering it off.

Hot Swapping. The ability to plug-in and begin using peripheral equipment without having to power off the computer first.

IEEE 1394. A hardware standard that provides high-bandwidth connections with peripheral devices that can sustain transfer rates as high as 400 Mbps.

Indexing. A Windows 2000 feature that allows it to build a searchable index based on the properties and contents of files located on local and network drives.

Internet Explorer. A free Internet browser included with Windows 2000 Professional.

IrDA. A secure wireless communications technology that uses the infrared protocol.

Last Known Good Configuration. A Windows 2000 startup option that allows the computer to be started using a previous configuration. This option is used to restart the computer when the current configuration has a problem.

Local Area Connection. A connection to a local area network that Windows 2000 automatically creates when it discovers an installed network interface card. These connections are stored on the Network and Dial-up Connections folder.

Locking a Computer. The process of placing the operating system in a state where no one but the currently logged on user or an administrator can access computer resources. The benefit of locking a computer is the user does not have to close all open applications and save all files and log off in order to secure the computer.

Log Off. The process of terminating a Windows session which includes saving all files and closing all open applications.

Log On. The process of validating an account name and password and gaining access to the computer and its resources.

Microsoft Management Consoles (MMC). A framework tool that contains management tools known as snap-ins from which you can administer your computer.

Microsoft Application Specification. A set of requirements that Microsoft has established that specifies the qualities a reliable Windows application must possess.

Microsoft Windows Logo. A logo software develops can display on their products if they meet the requirement of the Microsoft Application Specification.

Modem Sharing. The ability of Windows 2000 to provide shared access to other network computers to the Internet or other external networks. The computer that provides this service is also known as a proxy server.

MS-DOS. The original Microsoft operating system. It lacked integrated network support, security and a graphical user interface.

Multiple Monitor Support. A feature of Windows 2000 that allows between 2 to 9 monitors to be attached to a single computer.

My Computer. An icon on the Windows 2000 desktop that provides access to local drives and the Windows 2000 Professional Control Panel.

My Documents. An icon on the Windows 2000 desktop that provides access to a special folder where you can store all your personal files. A unique My Documents folder is created for each user of the computer and is only accessible by that user.

My Network Places. An icon on the Windows 2000 desktop that provides access to all network resources to which your computer is connected.

My Pictures. An icon on the Windows 2000 desktop that provides access to a special folder located inside your My Documents folder where you can store all of your graphic files and view them without having to open them.

Network Connection Wizard. A wizard that steps you through the process of establishing connections to every available type of network connection. Double clicking on the Make New Connection icon in the Network and Dial-up Connections folder starts it.

Network Drive. A disk drive or folder located on another network computer for which a drive mapping has been created allowing the remote resource to appear as if it were a local resource.

Network Identification Wizard. A wizard that helps you to connect your computer to a computer network.

Network interface card (NIC). A peripheral device that allows a computer to be connected to a network.

Network Place. A link to a network drive, web folder or FTP folder that is stored in the My Network Places folder.

New Technology File System (NTFS). A secure file system supported only by Windows NT and Windows 2000 operating systems which features support for advanced features such as NTFS security and encryption.

Outlook Express. An e-mail application supplied with Windows 2000 Professional.

Personalized Menus. A Windows 2000 feature which allows the operating system to adjust the Start Menu to the way you work by only displaying menu entries for the applications you use most often and hiding those which you seldom access.

Plug and Play. A feature that allows Windows 2000 to automatically detect, configure and manage peripheral devices.

Power Management. The ability of Windows 2000 to take control of your computer power consumption and adjust it based on current activity.

Power User. A Windows 2000 user account with the authority to install software and make configuration changes to the operating system.

Process. Windows applications are composed of one or more processes.

Proxy Modem Server. A computer that has been setup to provide access to a remote network to other computers via its modem.

Quick Launch toolbar. A toolbar located on the Windows 2000 Taskbar that provides single-lick access to applications such as Outlook Express and Internet Explorer.

Readiness Analyzer. A free utility available at the Microsoft web site that helps to determine if your computer is ready to support Windows 2000.

Recovery Console. A command line interface that allows you to start and stop services and write to local disk drives that are used to try and fix a Windows 2000 computer that fails to boot up.

Recycle Bin. The location where Windows 2000 sends file that you wish to delete. Files marked for deletion remain there until it begins to fill up. At which time Windows begins deleting files based on age. You can manually empty the Recycle Bin at any time.

Safe Mode. A special startup mode used to troubleshoot computer problems during startup. Pressing the F8 key during startup activates it.

Shutdown. The process of safely shutting down Windows 2000 before powering off the computer.

Smart Battery. A technology used by Windows 2000 Professional that allows the operating system to reduce power to unused hardware resources in an effort to extend the life of batteries.

Snap-in. A management application that runs within a Microsoft Management Console. It provides the ability to manage a specific Windows 2000 component or feature.

Standby. The ability of Windows to save your current working environment in memory placing your computer into a low power consumption state. The computer is automatically returned to its previous state when the user presses any key or clicks on the mouse.

Start Menu. The starting point for access to most Windows 2000 resources usually located in the lower right hand corner of the display.

Synchronize. The process of reconciling the offline files with their network counterparts.

Taskbar. A component on the Windows 2000 desktop which contains the Start Menu, System Tray, various toolbars and icons for active applications.

Task Manager. A utility that allows you to view the status of system resources and to manage applications and processes.

Thumbnail Views. The ability to display a miniature view of graphic files in Windows folders allowing you to view them without opening them.

Toolbar. A feature found on Windows applications, folders and utilities that provides single click access to a commonly used command or feature.

Troubleshooter. A specialized software utility that steps you through the process of resolving common problems on Windows computer.

Upgrade Pack. A special software program provided by application vendors that once installed enable earlier versions of their software to work properly on Windows 2000.

Upgrade Report. A report that you can run to determine if your computer is able to support the installation of Windows 2000.

Universal Serial BUS (USB). A new plug and play technology that allows multiple devices to be connected to the computer using a small USB cable. USB devices are able to share system resources and include such devices as scanners and digital cameras.

Utility. A Windows 2000 software program that performs a specific function and is not as robust as a complete software application.

VGA Mode. A special boot-mode that you can use to start Windows 2000 Professional and troubleshoot problems. When in this mode only a base set of software drivers are loaded.

Virtual Private Network (VPN). A secure virtual network established over another network such as the Internet.

Windows 2000 Professional. Microsoft's new operating system targeted at businesses and power users.

Windows 3.1. Microsoft's original 16-bit graphical environment that was loaded on MS-DOS based computers.

Windows Installer. A new software installation system that works behind the scenes to install and protect any compatible software applications installed on Windows 2000.

Windows NT Workstation 4. The name of the previous version of Windows 2000.

Windows NT Workstation 5. The original name of Windows 2000.

Windows Update. A utility that connects your computer to Microsoft's Windows 2000 web site, analyzes your system and presents you with a list of updates, service packs, software fixes, and updated software drivers.

Wizard. A software utility that steps the users through the process of performing a Windows task.

INDEX

A

Accelerated Graphics Port (AGP), 13, 89-90

Accessories, 36, 61, 94, 102, 127, 133

Account Name, 27, 38, 119, 136

Active Desktop, 9, 18, 56-58, 74, 81, 133

Active Desktop Gallery, 57, 81, 133

Add New Programs, 96, 98

Add Printer Wizard, 109-110, 114

Add/Remove Programs, 15-16, 96-97

Add/Remove Windows Components, 99

Address Toolbar, 69

Adjust Date/Time, 71-72

Administering User Accounts, 118

Administrator, xiii, 7, 27, 32-33, 37, 43, 110, 118, 123, 128, 133, 136

Advanced Power Management, 3, 12-13, 133

Application, 10, 14-15, 17, 19, 21, 26-27, 44-45, 49, 51, 59-61, 63, 67, 70, 89, 92, 94-97, 99-103, 105-108, 133, 137-138, 140-141

AutoComplete, 5, 67, 133

B

Backup Operators, 121

BIOS, 13-14, 89, 91, 134

Boot.ini, 46, 134

Boot Menu, 45-48, 134

Border, 79, 103

C

Calendar, 71
Change or Remove Programs, 96
Change Password, 42
Changing Backgrounds, 75
Changing Time Zones, 72
Connections to Private Networks, 8
Control Panel, 14, 36, 38, 40, 46, 51, 58-59, 63, 68, 74, 90, 96, 119, 124, 134, 137
Create Shortcut Wizard, 53

D

Date and Time, 71-73
Desktop, xiii-2, 9, 18-19, 21, 34, 36, 49-53, 56-58, 69-71, 74-76, 79-84, 86, 89, 91-92, 100-101, 104, 106, 133-134, 137, 140
Desktop Components, 49
Desktop Icons, 51, 58, 69, 84
Desktop Toolbar, 69
Direct Connections, 8
Disk Quotas, 24-25, 134
Display, 30, 37, 40, 47, 56-58, 64, 68, 71, 74-75, 77, 86-92, 94, 106, 125, 137, 140
Dual-boot, 24-26, 30, 46, 134
DVD, 13, 135

E

Encryption, 24-25, 134, 138
Empty Recycle Bin, 54, 139
Establishing An Automatic Login, 119

F

FAT, 24-25, 30, 135
FAT32, 24-25, 135
Favorites, 64-66
File, 1, 4-5, 23-25, 30-31, 46, 48, 51, 53-54, 61-62, 64, 67, 95, 104, 114, 134-135, 138-139
Folder, 6, 26, 51-52, 58-59, 61-62, 67, 70, 101, 103-104, 114, 133-138

G

Guest, 32-33, 118, 135

H

Hardware Compatibility List (HCL), 11
Hardware Requirements, 19, 23
Help, xiii, 16, 34-36, 39, 47, 59, 64-66, 87, 94-95, 100, 103, 127-128
Hibernation, 14, 135
High Color, 86
History, 45, 103
Hot Docking, 14, 135
Hot Swapping, 13-14, 135

I

Indexing, 5, 136
Incoming Connections, 8
IEEE 1394, 13, 136
Internet Connection, 8, 10, 36, 52, 57, 99, 127-128
Internet Explorer, 9-10, 18, 35, 52, 58, 61, 69, 81, 129, 136, 139
IrDA, 13, 136
Installing Windows 2000 Professional, 23, 27, 61, 101

T

Taskbar, 37, 50, 59, 61-63, 68-71, 92, 101, 106, 139-140
Taskbar & Start menu, 37, 50, 59, 61-63, 68, 101, 140
Task Manager, 43-45, 106-108, 140
Title Bar, 102, 106
Toolbar, 5, 69-70, 101, 103, 139-140
Troubleshooter, 87, 140
True Color, 86
Turning on a Screen Saver, 77

U

Universal Serial Bus (USB), 12-13
Upgrade Pack, 21, 26, 140
Upgrade Report, 26, 30, 140
User and Passwords, 119-120, 123
Utility, 9, 11-12, 14-16, 18, 43, 45, 51, 59, 63, 90, 96, 119-120, 123-124, 133, 139-141

V

Virtual Private Network (VPN), 8
VGA Mode, 47-48, 141
Volume Control, 70-71

W

Wallpaper, 75
Web Help, 66
Web Integration, 81-82
Windows 2000 Help Viewer, 64

www.ingramcontent.com/pod-product-compliance
Lightning Source LLC
Chambersburg PA
CBHW051242050326
40689CB00007B/1030